GINO'S

ITALIAN ESCAPE

HODDER &
STOUGHTON

GINO D'ACAMPO

I want to dedicate this book to my late father,
Ciro D'Acampo, who always used to say to me
'stop dreaming and get on with it'

First published in Great Britain in 2013
by Hodder & Stoughton
An Hachette UK company

I

Television series *Gino's Italian Escape* copyright
© ITV Studios Limited 2013. Licensed by ITV
Ventures Ltd. All rights reserved.

Recipes copyright © Gino D'Acampo 2013

Photography copyright © Matt Russell 2013,
except page 7 (private collection) and pages
2, 8, 13, 15, 19, 24, 28, 32, 49, 54, 58, 72, 84,
86, 96, 103, 107, 116, 119, 125, 131, 132, 148, 164,
172, 176, 198, 210, 218, 235, 248, 252, 259, 260,
270, 281 by Matt Russell, copyright © ITV Studios
Limited 2013

A CIP catalogue record for this title is available
from the British Library.

Hardback ISBN 978 1 444 75172 7
Ebook ISBN 978 1 444 75173 4

Design by Georgia Vaux

Typeset in Neutra Text and Mostra Nuova

Printed and bound in Germany by Mohn media

Hodder & Stoughton policy is to use papers that
are natural, renewable and recyclable products
and made from wood grown in sustainable
forests. The logging and manufacturing processes
are expected to conform to the environmental
regulations of the country of origin.

Hodder & Stoughton Ltd
338 Euston Road
London NW1 3BH

www.hodder.co.uk

ACKNOWLEDGEMENTS

A big thank you goes to my wife Jess and my kids,
for making every day of my life so fantastico!

To my best friend Marco Silvagni, my manager
Jeremy Hicks and everybody at Jeremy Hicks
Associates and Bonta' Italia.

A big kiss to everyone at Hodder & Stoughton
for trusting me to write this book with them – you
guys are great fun.

Grazie to Matt Russell, Georgia Vaux, Laura Fyfe
and Gee Charman for making sure that the book
and food looked beautiful.

To everybody at ITV for giving me the opportunity
to go around Italy filming the series and once
again trusting me to work with them.

The BIGGEST THANK YOU goes to my loyal fans,
for all the continuous support that you have
shown me in the past 10 years.

Buon appetito!

Gino xxx

INTRODUCTION
6

ANTIPASTI & APERITIVI
11

SOUPS
47

PASTA
65

PIZZA
101

MEAT
129

MEAT-FREE
161

FISH
185

SIDES & SALADS
207

BREADS & BISCUITS
229

DESSERTS
257

INDEX
286

* * * * * * * * * * * * * * *

ITALY IS MY HOMELAND. The land where I grew up as a child and the land that shapes the way I cook and eat today.

Food was always a huge part of my childhood. My grandfather was head chef at Costa Cruises, so I grew up with good food and knowing the importance of good-quality ingredients.

I hated school and am quite happy to admit that I hardly ever went, but at the age of 13 I found my direction in life: *food*. I enrolled at the Luigi de Medici catering college in Naples and finally found somewhere I wanted to attend every day. Being surrounded by food and cooking all day just seemed so natural.

After finishing college and working in Italy for a bit, I decided that I needed to venture to pastures new. When I was 20 years old I moved to London to work in restaurants and forge my career in food.

The UK is now my home and where my family live, but I still have firm roots in Italy. I guess there are two reasons for this. First, traditions and food culture are bred into every Italian, and living in a different country, even for 16 years, will never dilute them – I still cook Italian food every day and we are lucky enough to visit Italy on family holidays. Second, Italian cuisine, with its emphasis on simple, good-quality ingredients enjoyed in the company of family and friends, is such a simple formula that it works wherever you are in the world.

When I do venture back to Italy, family is always at the forefront of my mind. In true Italian style many of my close relatives still live in the area where we grew up. Aunts live next door or close to my cousins, grandparents live within walking distance of their grandchildren, and doors are left open for the family to gather in whichever house happens to be at the heart of the family on that particular day or with whoever has a pot of pasta boiling away.

I love going back there to see everybody, and when filming for my TV series I finally got to cook for them. Believe it or not, I have never cooked for my extended family. If they come to the UK, they want to sample the various amazing restaurants we have here (they are unlikely to find a curry house in Torre del Greco), and if we go to Italy, they want to cook for me. So this was my opportunity to cook for them and, to be honest, I was a little nervous about it. Cooking in other people's kitchens can sometimes be a bit awkward but the famous Italian hospitality means that they are offended if you don't treat their house as your own – mess and all!

Family is at the centre of any Italian table, and this was especially brought home to me on my various adventures around the south of Italy, from the lemon groves on the Amalfi coast, where Salvatore and his family

* * * * * * * * * * * * * * *

both grew the lemons and made limoncello from them, to Casolare da Tobia, the family-run restaurant on the volcano crater just outside the city of Naples.

Families eat together and work together. Generations of the same family work side by side, taking responsibility for their own products but also sharing the burden of everyday life. This was so apparent at the cherry orchard in Castello, where Ciro worked on his area of land and his brothers on the other plots but they all shared the workers who sorted and stacked the cherries. A true family business.

Not surprisingly, in a country where food plays such a prominent role, meals in Italy can be rather elaborate affairs and we like to take our time. We have courses, as in England, but are slightly stricter about what can be served in each. We start with an *aperitivo*, or aperitif, often accompanied by nibbles. This is nearly always followed by *antipasto*, which is usually (but not always) a cold starter of cured meats, cheeses, vegetables and salads. We will then have our *primo* (first course), often a pasta, soup or risotto option. Still hungry? OK, now we enjoy our *secondo* (main course), traditionally the heartiest part of the meal, which will always be either fish or meat. And if you can still fit it in, there's dessert and coffee, followed by a *digestivo*, or liqueur. Now you know why we go for siestas after lunch!

It's sometimes difficult to generalise about Italian food because Italy is made up of 20 regions and every town or village makes the same dish in very different ways. Local cooking is shaped by geographic, historical and climatic differences, and today's Italian cuisine is the result of the slow integration of the country's many different regional traditions and food customs. When Italy was unified in the mid-19th century, only about

TORRE DEL GRECO

*　*　*　*　*　*　*　*　*　*　*　*　*　*　*

2 per cent of the total population was able to speak and understand the national language – instead they spoke their own regional dialects. The same kind of separation was also reflected in the food.

Food in Italy is still very regional and each area is known for specific dishes, ingredients and pasta shapes. Bari, for example, is noted for its orecchiette, and you can still see women sitting in the cobbled streets of the old town making it by hand. Gragnano, by comparison, is known for fusilli, made by rolling linguine around a long, thin metal rod, traditionally an umbrella spoke. It is still rolled by hand to this day, and I have to say it is easier than making orecchiette by hand – I have tried both. Speed was not on my side and the factory definitely wouldn't give me a job!

The obvious accompaniment to all this is, of course, wine. Italians love good wine but I would never consider them to be binge drinkers. They enjoy a good glass or two with their meal but I've very rarely seen family members past the point of no return. Wine becomes an important part of celebrations and family meals from a young age and, as always, we prefer quality over quantity.

Like the food, wine in Italy is also regional. There are vineyards all over the country, growing more than 350 different grape varieties, from traditional southern whites, such as Catarratto and Fiano, to the 'noble' variety of Aglianico, a delicious red.

As a general rule, northern Italian wines tend to have lighter flavours than those from the south, where the stronger sun results in bigger, bolder flavours, as in New World wines. But, as always in Italy, the cuisine in each region reflects the wine and grape variety grown there. So if you are in Puglia, eating traditional cuisine, a good rule is to go for a grape variety grown in Puglia.

Simplicity itself. And that's the key to Italian cuisine. Fresh, top-quality seasonal ingredients cooked simply to allow the flavours to speak for themselves. When travelling for *Gino's Italian Escape*, I was struck time and again by the passion and commitment to quality shown by the food producers I met, and how they have continued to preserve the timeless family traditions that make Italian cuisine what it is. In the face of such amazing producers it was difficult not to come up with amazing recipes for the book. I couldn't help but feel inspired. I hope you are too.

ANTIPASTI & APERITIVI

✳ ✳ ✳ ✳ ✳ ✳ ✳ ✳ ✳ ✳ ✳ ✳ ✳ ✳ ✳ ✳

ANTIPASTO (PLURAL *ANTIPASTI*) ACTUALLY MEANS 'before the meal', and is what Italians traditionally eat before the first course. I guess it's similar to serving canapés, but instead of standing and mingling with guests, you help yourself, buffet-style, while seated at the table.

I'll never forget the first time I took my wife to Naples and we sat down for dinner. She tucked into the antipasti, not realising that a pasta, then a meat or fish dish, were to follow. I know it was a bit mean not to tell her but I still remember the look on her face after devouring loads of antipasti and bread, only to learn this wasn't even the starter – hilarious. I love Italian meals like this. How wonderful to actually take time out to sit around a table with family or friends and spend hours together chatting and enjoying great food. Absolute heaven!

Antipasti vary but usually consist of some kind of plated cured meats accompanied by seasonal vegetables such as olives, peperoncini, mushrooms, caper berries and artichoke hearts, plus anchovies, various cheeses, such as provolone or mozzarella (see my guide on page 14) and pickled vegetables (in oil or vinegar). The choices on offer will vary according to region. In southern Italy antipasti will include different preparations of saltwater fish and traditional southern cured meats; in the north, there will be different kinds of cured meats; and near lakes, freshwater fish will be served. The cheeses on offer also vary significantly between regions, from creamy smooth buffalo mozzarella in Naples to amazing pecorino from Sardinia.

Cured meats for antipasti may include mortadella (a clear favourite with my children), but, more traditionally, smoked ham, types of salami, prosciutto and coppa are usually offered, according to preference (see my guide on page 15 and also chapter 5, page 130). The great joy of antipasti is that you can choose whatever you like. This really is a case of anything goes.

I never have a dinner party without offering an antipasti selection. My guests now expect it and have learnt not to fill themselves up too much on what's on offer.

An aperitivo is, plainly and simply, a pre-dinner drink, meant to open the palate and give you a chance to socialise, relax, and enjoy some nibbles as dinner approaches. The aperitivo and its popularity has changed dramatically over the years. Italians (like many people all over the world) used to perhaps pop briefly into their local bar after work for the odd Campari or Aperol, or they might have their little fix at home before their meal, but now the aperitivo is a trend that everyone seems to be embracing and a new craze has been born. During the early evening most bars in large cities serve aperitivi with complimentary food. We're not talking 'Happy Hour' here. These drinks are not cheap, but usually have an added supplement for the food being served, which can often consist of hefty portions of antipasti that you just help yourself to at the bar. In fact, bars in Italy are now competing to see who can offer the best and most free food.

Italian working hours are different from those in many other countries and cultures: people often start work at 8 a.m. and go home around 12.30 p.m. for a huge lunch and a siesta. They then return to work at around 4 p.m. and work until 8 p.m. I guess if you have had a large meal at lunch and it's a nice evening, why would you want to go home after a long day at work, especially if you've had a nap in the afternoon? Meeting your friends and family and going to a small deli or bar where you can enjoy a few glasses of whatever takes your fancy and some fresh local produce sounds extremely tempting to me.

What I really love about the owners of bars, delis or restaurants in Italy, is how passionate they are about what they have to offer, why it's the best and how it's made. Even if you are not that interested in food, you can't help but get swept away in their enthusiasm, and you quite often come out having learnt something about cheese, meat or wine that you never knew before. What a perfect way to spend an evening.

✳ ✳ ✳ ✳ ✳ ✳ ✳ ✳ ✳ ✳ ✳ ✳ ✳ ✳ ✳ ✳

GINO'S GUIDE TO MOZZARELLA

Originally from southern Italy, mozzarella is a versatile cheese that comes in many different types. Here's my personal guide.

LOW-MOISTURE MOZZARELLA – This has had some of its water removed so it does not 'leak' when cooked. Perfect for pizzas, as it prevents them from going soggy.

MOZZARELLA AFFUMICATA – Smoked mozzarella, perfect for wrapping in pancetta and frying.

MOZZARELLA DI BUFALA – Made from water buffalo milk, perfectly soft and creamy but with a high moisture content. Perfect for salads and for my Marinated Mozzarella recipe on page 37.

MOZZARELLA FIOR DI LATTE – Made from pasteurised cow's milk and cheaper than the buffalo milk version. (In the UK if the packet does not state that it is buffalo mozzarella, you can assume it is made from cow's milk.

GINO'S GUIDE TO CURED MEATS

Here are the most popular meats that would normally be offered as antipasti – and my personal favourites.

BRESAOLA – Air-dried beef with a deep red colour, this sweet-flavoured meat is served thinly sliced in salads and sandwiches.

CAPOCOLLO – Fully air-dried, thinly cut pork shoulder or neck, seasoned with spicy red pepper, capocollo is from the Campania region. It is the southern equivalent of coppa, a traditional ham from Emilia-Romagna.

MORTADELLA – An Italian spice-flavoured sausage made from pork neck. The traditional version from Bologna contains black pepper and myrtle.

PANCETTA – This salt-cured pork belly is seasoned with nutmeg, pepper, fennel, dried ground hot peppers, and garlic. It is served thinly sliced or chopped after a three-month drying process.

PROSCIUTTO – A sweet-flavoured ham, most famously from Parma. Its intensive curing process includes rubbing and salting by hand, followed by long periods of air-drying. It's normally served uncooked, as prosciutto crudo. (The cooked version is known as prosciutto cotto.)

BRUSCHETTE CON PESTO DI POMODORI SECCHI
BRUSCHETTE WITH SUN-DRIED TOMATO PESTO

Bruschette are eaten all over Italy, and we all know and love the traditional tomato-based recipe – I, for one, certainly grew up on it. This version just adds a little twist to the classic dish and is perfect for entertaining.

Serves 4 as a starter

1 CIABATTA LOAF, CUT INTO SLICES
    2CM THICK
2 TABLESPOONS OLIVE OIL
1 GARLIC CLOVE, PEELED AND HALVED
5–6 TOMATOES, DESEEDED AND DICED
FRESH BASIL LEAVES AND PARMESAN
    CHEESE SHAVINGS TO GARNISH

For the pesto

150G SUN-DRIED TOMATOES IN OIL,
    DRAINED
1 GARLIC CLOVE, PEELED
SMALL BUNCH OF FRESH BASIL
2 TABLESPOONS PINE NUTS
3 TABLESPOONS OLIVE OIL
2 TABLESPOONS FRESHLY GRATED
    PARMESAN CHEESE
SALT AND BLACK PEPPER TO TASTE

First make the pesto. Place the sun-dried tomatoes, garlic, basil and pine nuts in a small food processor and blitz until you have a rough paste. Add the olive oil and Parmesan and blitz again until smooth. Season and set to one side.

To make the bruschette, heat a griddle pan over a high heat. Brush the ciabatta slices with a little olive oil, then pop them on the griddle for 1–2 minutes until charred on both sides. Remove from the pan and rub one side of each slice with the cut side of the garlic.

Spread a little of the pesto on each bruschetta, then scatter with a few of the diced tomatoes.

Serve topped with a few basil leaves and Parmesan shavings.

BRUSCHETTE CON PESTO DI POMODORI SECCHI

COCKTAIL CON LIMONCELLO

LIMONCELLO COCKTAIL

Limoncello in Italy is served as a digestive after a big meal but I think it is just as good in a cocktail. Salvatore and his family, who owned the lemon grove I recently visited, make their own limoncello and were quite adamant that once a bottle has been opened, it should be stored in the fridge and not, as so many people do, in the freezer. So go and get your opened bottle out of the freezer and make this cocktail, even if it is a Monday night. Then, on the orders of Salvatore, put the bottle back in the fridge!

~~~~~~~~~~~~~~~~~~~~~~~~~~~~~~~

Serves 6

½ LEMON

2 TABLESPOONS CASTER SUGAR

6 TABLESPOONS LIMONCELLO

1 BOTTLE OF CHILLED PROSECCO

Take 6 champagne flutes and run the cut side of the lemon around the rim of each glass just to wet it a little. Put the sugar on a plate and dip the rim of each glass in it to frost the edge.

Pour a tablespoon of limoncello into each glass and top up with Prosecco. Serve straight away.

COCKTAIL CON LIMONCELLO

ROTOLINI DI PROSCIUTTO CRUDO E MOZZARELLA

ROTOLINI DI PROSCIUTTO CRUDO E MOZZARELLA

Mozzarella and Parma Ham Rolls

When guests unexpectedly turn up at that awkward time between late afternoon and supper, a glass of wine is quite acceptable, but it is always nice to be able to give them a little something to eat as well. These rolls use ingredients that I always have in my fridge, and they are super-quick to make.

If you are ever lucky enough to get hold of fresh mozzarella like the one I found at the Vannulo farm, just eat it as it stands. If, though, you get your mozzarella from the supermarket, this is the perfect recipe as it gives it just a bit of a flavour boost.

~~~~~~~~~~~~~~~~~~~~~~~~

Makes 8 rolls

4 TABLESPOONS CREAM CHEESE
2 TABLESPOONS PESTO (SEE PAGE 73)
8 SLICES OF PROSCIUTTO

1 BALL OF MOZZARELLA, DRAINED AND CUT INTO STRIPS
70G ROCKET LEAVES

Mix together the cream cheese and pesto. Season with black pepper.

Lay the slices of prosciutto on a clean board. Carefully spread a little of the cream cheese mixture on each one. Place a small bunch of rocket leaves at one end of each slice, allowing the tips of them to poke out. Top with a strip of mozzarella, then carefully roll up the prosciutto.

Serve with a glass of chilled wine or a Limoncello Cocktail (see page 18).

ARANCINI CON SALSA DI POMODORI ARROSTITI

RICE BALLS WITH ROASTED TOMATO AND PEPPER SAUCE

Arancini are deep-fried risotto balls that can be stuffed with mozzarella or ragù (sauce). Their name – which comes from *arancia*, the Italian word for 'orange' – means 'little oranges'. These delicious rice balls originate from Sicily and are served in cafés all over the island. In recent years they have become a popular kind of Italian street food and are perfect for using up leftover risotto.

~~~~~~~~~~~~~~~~~~

Serves 4

25G DRIED PORCINI MUSHROOMS

4 TABLESPOONS OLIVE OIL, PLUS
  EXTRA FOR DRIZZLING

½ AN ONION, PEELED AND CHOPPED

400G ARBORIO RICE

400ML VEGETABLE STOCK

150G FRESHLY GRATED PARMESAN
  CHEESE

3 EGGS, SEPARATED, WHITES LIGHTLY
  BEATEN

200G MOZZARELLA CHEESE, CUBED

100G PLAIN FLOUR

200G TOASTED FINE BREADCRUMBS

ABOUT 1 LITRE VEGETABLE OIL, FOR
  DEEP-FRYING

SALT AND BLACK PEPPER TO TASTE

PARMESAN SHAVINGS AND FRESH
  BASIL LEAVES TO GARNISH

For the tomato and pepper sauce

3 RED PEPPERS

4 TOMATOES, HALVED

1 GARLIC CLOVE, PEELED AND SLICED

3 TABLESPOONS OLIVE OIL

Soak the dried mushrooms in boiling water.

Meanwhile, heat the olive oil in a heavy-based saucepan over a medium heat and gently fry the onion until softened. Add the rice and fry for 3 minutes, stirring constantly. Add a ladleful of the stock, season and cook, stirring all the time, until the liquid is absorbed.

Continue to add ladlefuls of stock in the same way. When half has been added, drain the mushrooms, pouring their liquid (minus any grit) into the rice. Continue adding the remaining stock until it has all been used and

ROME

the rice is cooked through but still has a slight bite (this should take about 18 minutes). Add more water if necessary to complete the cooking process.

Finely chop the soaked mushrooms, then mix them into the rice along with the Parmesan cheese and the 3 egg yolks. Season with salt and pepper, then spread the rice mixture onto a tray and leave to cool.

Once cooled, take 2 tablespoons of the rice mixture in your hands and press together. Push a piece of mozzarella into the centre of the rice and mould the rice around it, making a ball.

Put the flour and breadcrumbs on separate plates. Dip the rice ball first into the flour, then the egg white, coating it thoroughly, and finally in the breadcrumbs. Repeat the process until all the rice has been used up.

Place the rice balls on a tray and refrigerate for 1 hour to firm up.

Meanwhile, make the sauce. Preheat the oven to 180°C/gas mark 4. Cut the peppers in half, discarding the seeds and stalks, and place in a baking tray. Add the tomatoes and garlic, a good glug of olive oil, and season with salt and pepper. Roast for 40 minutes or until the peppers are soft.

When cooked, place everything in a blender and blitz until smooth. Season with salt and pepper.

Heat a deep-fat fryer to 190°C, or heat the oil in a deep pan until a cube of bread dropped in the hot oil sizzles and turns brown in 30 seconds. Make sure the oil is deep enough to completely cover the arancini.

Deep-fry the arancini in batches for 1–2 minutes until golden brown and hot in the middle. (This will depend on how big they are, so you might need to test one.) Remove with a slotted spoon and drain on kitchen paper.

Serve each freshly fried arancini topped with 2–3 tablespoons of your red pepper sauce, Parmesan shavings, basil leaves and a drizzle of olive oil.

PEPERONI AL FORNO CON ACCIUGHE E PINOLI

ROASTED PEPPERS WITH ANCHOVIES AND PINE NUTS

This almost doesn't qualify as cooking because the recipe is so easy. It uses the best of Italian ingredients and its beauty lies in its simplicity. The peppers become sweet when roasted, creating a delicious juice that is perfect for mopping up with large chunks of Italian bread.

~~~~~~~~~~~~~~~~~~~~~~~~~

Serves 4

2 YELLOW PEPPERS
12 CHERRY TOMATOES
8 ANCHOVY FILLETS IN OIL, DRAINED
OLIVE OIL
25G PINE NUTS

SALT AND BLACK PEPPER TO TASTE
FRESH BASIL LEAVES AND PARMESAN
 SHAVINGS TO GARNISH
GOOD-QUALITY THICK BALSAMIC
 VINEGAR AND BREAD TO SERVE

Preheat the oven to 180°C/gas mark 4.

Cut the peppers in half lengthways, going straight through the stalk if you can. Discard the cord and seeds, then lay the halved peppers on a baking tray. Cut the tomatoes in half and divide them between the peppers. Top with a couple of anchovy fillets, drizzle with olive oil and season with black pepper. Place in the oven for 20 minutes until the peppers are tender.

While the peppers are cooking, lightly toast the pine nuts in a dry frying pan for a couple of minutes, then transfer them to a plate.

Tear some basil leaves and scatter them over the cooked peppers, then sprinkle the pine nuts and a few Parmesan shavings on top.

Serve drizzled with balsamic vinegar and a little more olive oil.

PEPERONI AL FORNO CON ACCIUGHE E PINOLI

AMALFI

GAMBERONI E CALAMARI GRIGLIATI CON MAYONNAISE AL LIMONE

GAMBERONI E CALAMARI GRIGLIATI CON MAYONNAISE AL LIMONE

GRIDDLED PRAWNS AND SQUID WITH CHILLI AND LEMON MAYONNAISE

The coastal regions of Italy love their seafood. This is a delicious and simple recipe in which everything can be prepared the night before and then simply griddled or placed on the barbecue.

∿∿∿∿∿∿∿∿∿∿∿∿∿

Serves 4

8 BABY SQUID, CLEANED

12 LARGE UNSHELLED KING PRAWNS

2 GARLIC CLOVES, PEELED AND SLICED

3 TABLESPOONS OLIVE OIL

2 FRESH ROSEMARY SPRIGS

SALT AND BLACK PEPPER TO TASTE

For the mayonnaise

2 FREE RANGE EGG YOLKS

½ TEASPOON DIJON MUSTARD

ZEST OF 1 LEMON AND JUICE OF ½

½ RED CHILLI, DESEEDED AND FINELY CHOPPED

300ML OLIVE OIL

Cut your cleaned squid down the middle, opening them up like a book. Lay them flat on a board and lightly score the flesh in a diamond pattern, taking care not to cut right through it.

Place the squid and prawns in a plastic bag along with the garlic, olive oil and rosemary. Shake everything together, then place in the fridge for 2 hours or, better still, overnight.

To make the mayonnaise, place the egg yolks, mustard and lemon juice in a blender. Blitz for 15 seconds, then slowly, with the motor running, pour in the oil. Once all the oil has been added, season the mayonnaise with salt and pepper, add the zest and a little more lemon juice if needed. Place in the fridge until needed.

Once the prawns have marinated, remove the bag from the fridge at least 30 minutes before cooking.

Heat a griddle pan over a high heat. Place the prawns on it and cook for 3 minutes on each side until pink. Transfer to a serving platter. Place the squid on the griddle pan and cook for 1 minute – it will curl up.

Add the squid to the prawn platter and serve with the lemon and chilli mayonnaise.

CARTA DI MUSICA CON SPEZIE E PESTATA DI OLIVE

Spiced Paper-thin Bread with Olive Tapenade

These delicately thin breads – their name translates literally as 'music paper' – are the perfect start to a meal, especially alongside a glass of chilled Prosecco. They are ideal to play around with, as you can spice them with whatever takes your fancy.

~~~~~~~~~~~~~~~~~~~~~~

Makes 8 breads

200G WHITE FLOUR,
 TYPE '00'
100G FINE SEMOLINA
GOOD PINCH OF SALT
OLIVE OIL

To spice the breads:
FENNEL SEEDS (LIGHTLY
CRUSHED), PAPRIKA, GROUND
 CUMIN, CAYENNE PEPPER,
 GROUND BLACK PEPPER,
 SEA SALT

For the tapenade
1 GARLIC CLOVE, PEELED
JUICE OF 1 LEMON
1 TABLESPOON SALTED CAPERS,
 RINSED
6 ANCHOVY FILLETS IN OIL,
 DRAINED
PINCH OF DRIED CHILLI
 FLAKES (OPTIONAL)
250G PITTED BLACK OLIVES
SMALL BUNCH OF FRESH
 PARSLEY
3 TABLESPOONS OLIVE OIL

Preheat the oven to 200°C/gas mark 6.

Put the flour, semolina and salt into a bowl and combine with 200ml water. Knead to a smooth dough, then divide into 10 equal pieces.

Now this is where you can use some machine or muscle power. Pass each piece of dough through a floured pasta machine, or roll out by hand, into long thin sheets. Pop each sheet onto a non-stick baking tray.

Brush each sheet lightly with olive oil, then scatter with the spice of your choice. (I like to make a few different types, some with crushed fennel seeds, some with sea salt and some with paprika.)

Place the breads in the oven and cook for 4–5 minutes until golden and crispy. (They cook really quickly, so no going off to make a cup of tea!) Once cooked, remove from the oven and leave to cool.

To make the tapenade, place the ingredients, apart from the olive oil and black pepper, in a blender and blitz until you have a rough paste. Drizzle in the olive oil to loosen the mixture and blend once more.

Serve your paper-thin breads with the tapenade handed separately.

MOZZARELLA SFIZIOSA

MOZZARELLA SFIZIOSA

Marinated Mozzarella Balls

When you think of Italy, two cheeses immediately spring to mind: Parmesan and mozzarella. This recipe puts mozzarella centre stage with two different marinades that are guaranteed to impress.

Serves 4

2 BUFFALO MOZZARELLA BALLS,
   DRAINED
MARINATED ARTICHOKES
MARINATED VEGETABLES
MIXED OLIVES
CAPER BERRIES
A SELECTION OF ITALIAN CURED
   MEATS
TOASTED CIABATTA BREAD TO SERVE

For marinade 1
½ LARGE RED CHILLI, DESEEDED
SMALL BUNCH OF FRESH PARSLEY

SMALL BUNCH OF FRESH MINT
2 TABLESPOONS EXTRA VIRGIN
   OLIVE OIL
SALT TO TASTE

For marinade 2
½ SMALL GARLIC CLOVE, PEELED
1 TEASPOON FRESH THYME LEAVES
½ TEASPOON FRESH OREGANO
   LEAVES
ZEST OF ½ UNWAXED LEMON
2 TABLESPOONS EXTRA VIRGIN
   OLIVE OIL

First make marinade 1. Finely chop the chilli, parsley and mint. Place in a bowl and add the olive oil. Season with salt.

To make marinade 2, place the garlic, thyme and oregano in a mortar, add a pinch of salt and use the pestle to grind them into a paste. Add the lemon zest and olive oil along with a little black pepper. Mix together and set to one side.

Place the drained mozzarella balls on a board or platter and cut a cross in the top of each one. Drizzle one with the chilli marinade and the other with the garlic marinade.

Serve the marinated mozzarella alongside the other antipasti ingredients, or just have them on their own with toasted bread and tomatoes.

FICHI AL FORNO CON RIPIENO DI RICOTTA AVVOLTI IN PANCETTA

FICHI AL FORNO CON RIPIENO DI RICOTTA AVVOLTI IN PANCETTA

Warm Figs Stuffed with Herb Ricotta and Wrapped in Pancetta

The natural sweetness of figs is enhanced when cooked, as here, to create a perfect complement to the saltiness of pancetta. Even if you're not normally a fan of sweet fruits and savoury meat together, I urge you to try this – it's truly delicious.

~~~~~~~~~~~~~~

Serves 4

8 FIGS, WASHED

100G RICOTTA CHEESE

1 TABLESPOON FINELY CHOPPED
 FRESH CHIVES

ZEST OF 1 UNWAXED LEMON

8 SLICES OF PANCETTA

3 TABLESPOONS RUNNY HONEY

A FEW FRESH THYME LEAVES

SALT AND BLACK PEPPER TO TASTE

GREEN SALAD TO SERVE

Preheat the oven to 180°C/gas mark 4. Cut a cross in the top of each fig, going about halfway down the flesh.

Mix the ricotta, chives and lemon zest together, then season with salt and pepper. Place a heaped teaspoon of the mixture inside each fig.

Wrap a slice of pancetta around each fig, then place on a baking tray and roast in the oven for 10 minutes, until the pancetta is crispy.

Warm the honey and thyme leaves in a small pan.

Serve the figs with a green salad and a drizzle of the warmed honey mixture.

FAGIOLI AL ROSMARINO CON PANE TOSTATO ALL'AGLIO

Italian Beans with Rosemary on Garlic Toasts

You might be tempted to think this recipe is just posh beans on toast, but to us Italians it's an important dish, especially in regions where beans are a staple part of the diet.

~~~~~~~~~~~~~~~~~~~~~~~~

Serves 4

8 SLICES OF CIABATTA BREAD
2 TABLESPOONS OLIVE OIL
1 GARLIC CLOVE, PEELED
SALT AND BLACK PEPPER TO TASTE
EXTRA VIRGIN OLIVE OIL TO SERVE

For the beans

2 TABLESPOONS EXTRA VIRGIN
  OLIVE OIL
1 RED ONION, PEELED AND THINLY
  SLICED
150G CHERRY TOMATOES, QUARTERED
2 TABLESPOONS COARSELY CHOPPED
  FLAT LEAF PARSLEY
2 X 400G TINS CANNELLINI BEANS,
  DRAINED AND RINSED

Heat a griddle pan over a high heat. Cover one side of each slice of bread with olive oil, then season with salt. Place the slices on the griddle for a few minutes until charred lines appear and the bread is crispy. Turn over and repeat on the other side.

While the bread is toasting, prepare the beans. Heat a frying pan over a medium heat, then add the oil and onion and season with salt. Cook for 5 minutes until softened. Add the tomatoes, cook for about a minute until they start to release their juices, then stir in the parsley.

Add the beans and cook for 2 minutes until warmed through, adding a litle water if the mixture seems dry. You do not want the beans to get mushy, so once cooked, remove from the heat and season well with black pepper.

When the ciabatta is done, rub one side with the garlic. Serve the beans on top of the toast and finish with a drizzle of olive oil.

PAGNOTTA RIPIENA

PICNIC PIE

While filming in Italy, we visited the amazing *trulli* houses of Alberobello. I had been to see these domed limestone dwellings as a child and was sure they must be where the Smurfs lived! We were lucky enough to be there for a local festival, and this was the ideal recipe to take, as it is perfect portable food. Stuff it with whatever veggies, cheeses or meats you fancy, but those listed below are my favourites.

~~~~~~~~~~~~~~~~~~~~~~~~~~

Serves 4

2 COURGETTES

2 TABLESPOONS EXTRA VIRGIN OLIVE OIL

1 ROUND CRUSTY LOAF OF BREAD

20 THIN SLICES OF SALAMI

100G CACIOCAVALLO OR CHEDDAR CHEESE, SLICED

1 X 280G JAR OF SUN-DRIED TOMATOES IN OIL, DRAINED

1 X 290G JAR OF PEPPERS IN OIL, DRAINED

SALT AND BLACK PEPPER TO TASTE

Heat a griddle pan over a high heat. Using a potato peeler, cut the courgettes into long thin strips. Drizzle with olive oil and season with salt and pepper. Place the strips on the griddle and cook on each side for 1 minute until charred stripes appear. Set aside on a plate to cool.

Cut the top off the loaf to create a lid. Use your hands to scoop out the dough inside. Line the base and sides of the hollowed-out loaf with the salami. Cover with a layer of cheese, followed by the tomatoes, courgette strips and peppers, seasoning between each layer with black pepper. Keep going, packing everything down tightly, until you have filled the entire loaf.

Replace the 'lid' on the loaf, wrap in cling film and refrigerate for up to 12 hours.

When ready to eat, unwrap the chilled loaf, cut into large wedges and enjoy on the go or at a picnic.

CROCCHE DI PATATE

CROCCHE DI PATATE

CROQUETTE POTATOES WITH HAM AND PARMESAN

There is something amazing about the combination of potato, cheese and ham that is taken to a new level when deep-fried. These are hot little parcels of pure pleasure.

~~~~~~~~~~~~~~~~~~~~~~~~~~~~

Serves 4/makes 12

500G UNPEELED FLOURY POTATOES

50G BUTTER

1 EGG YOLK

100G FRESHLY GRATED PARMESAN
  CHEESE

100G COOKED HAM, CHOPPED

150G PLAIN FLOUR

2 EGGS, BEATEN

250G FINE POLENTA

ABOUT 1 LITRE VEGETABLE OIL,
  FOR DEEP-FRYING

SALT AND BLACK PEPPER TO TASTE

Preheat the oven to 190°C/gas mark 5. Place the potatoes on a baking tray and bake in the oven for 1 hour until tender. When cooked, set aside to cool slightly., then scoop out the flesh and pop it into a bowl.

Mash the potato with the butter, then beat in the egg yolk, Parmesan and ham. Season well with salt and pepper.

Shape the mixture into 12 thick sausages. Roll these in the flour, then the beaten egg and finally the polenta. Dip them back into the egg and roll them in the polenta once more. Refrigerate for 1 hour or overnight.

Heat a deep-fat fryer to 190°C, or heat the oil in a deep pan until a cube of bread dropped in the hot oil sizzles and turns brown in 30 seconds. Fry the croquettes until golden brown and piping hot. When cooked, drain them on kitchen paper to remove the excess oil. Sprinklè with salt and serve hot.

SOUPS

'Anyone who tells a lie has not a pure heart, and cannot make a good soup'.
Ludwig van Beethoven

BEFORE I MOVED TO ENGLAND IN OCTOBER 1995, the only soup I had ever really had was minestrone, and because I come from a hot climate, it was never really a first-choice dish. But within my first week over here, I tasted an old-fashioned Jewish chicken soup and I was hooked. Of course, I had to change the original recipe to create my own twist but from then on, soup was on my hit list, and through the winter months it was a must-have.

Soup has always been with us. Roots, vegetables and meats were boiled in water that was initially discarded, but eventually it became fashionable to eat the liquid on its own, soaked up with bread, which was used as a spoon. (The word 'soup' is in fact said to come from the Latin word *suppare*, meaning 'to soak', which refers both to the bread that was soaked and to the broth itself.)

By the 16th century, soup was often used as a restorative for people who were sick, and this is still the case. (I know I can't prove it, but if you're feeling ill, try my Brodo di Gallina on page 56 – it works for me every time.) The health benefits of soup will vary, of course, depending on the ingredients, but if you steer clear of dairy products and eat soups made from fresh vegetables or beans, you will be guaranteed a great intake of protein, fibre, heart-healthy unsaturated fat, vitamins and minerals.

Essentially, any soup is a broth that is full of flavour. It can be crystal clear like a consommé, thick or smooth and creamy, or so chunky with meat, fish, grains or vegetables that it is just this side of a stew. (This is the case with Italian soups, such as minestrone or Neapolitan bean soup, which contain pasta, beans and pulses.)

Soup is the most versatile of dishes. It can be the first of several courses, intended just to whet the appetite; it can be one of many dishes served at the same time; or it can be a hearty meal in a bowl. You can make it a day in advance if necessary, then reheat it and serve with warm bread as a starter or a main course that is ready in just minutes.

In earlier times, soup was considered a frugal food in which stock or water allowed cheap pulses and small amounts of meat to be stretched out between large numbers of people. We have come a long way since then, and today soup can be as frugal or rich as you like, from a simple bean soup to a hearty fish one, but each has its place in any home.

* * * * * * * * * * * * * * * *

In this chapter I have chosen a few of my favourites to tempt you. And remember, with soup you can be as creative as you like. Anything (well, almost!) goes. Quite often, spontaneous soups are the best, but if you feel anxious about experimenting straight away, try my choices first to get you in the mood.

ZUPPA DI CIPOLLE E PANCETTA

ZUPPA DI CIPOLLE E PANCETTA

ONION, TOMATO AND PANCETTA SOUP

By far – and I really mean by far – this has to be my favourite soup recipe in any of my books. If you like onion soup, this is so much more – in fact, I don't know anyone who has tried it and not loved it. I think you will be amazed at the flavour combinations. Make sure it is always served hot. It will keep refrigerated for 48 hours, but remember, like most soups, it can be reheated only once.

~~~~~~~~~~~~~~~~~~~

Serves 4

4 TABLESPOONS EXTRA VIRGIN
   OLIVE OIL
250G DICED PANCETTA
700G WHITE ONIONS, PEELED AND
   FINELY SLICED
1.5 LITRES CHICKEN STOCK, MADE
   WITH STOCK CUBES

1 X 400G TIN CHOPPED TOMATOES
SALT AND BLACK PEPPER TO TASTE
4 TABLESPOONS FRESH PARMESAN
   CHEESE SHAVINGS, 6 FRESH BASIL
   LEAVES AND WARM CRUSTY BREAD
   TO SERVE

Place a large saucepan over a medium heat, pour in the oil and fry the pancetta for 3 minutes, stirring constantly with a wooden spoon.

Add the onions and stir everything together. Lower the heat and cook for 20 minutes, stirring occasionally. When the onions are a beautiful golden colour, pour in the stock and tomatoes. Bring to the boil, then lower the heat, half-cover the pan and simmer for 40 minutes, stirring occasionally.

About 5 minutes before the cooking time is up, check the consistency of the soup and add a little more water if it is too thick.

Just before serving, taste and season with salt and pepper, if needed (the pancetta may already have added enough saltiness).

Serve hot, with Parmesan shavings and basil leaves sprinkled on top, and slices of warm crusty bread.

MINESTRONE

CHUNKY VEGETABLE SOUP WITH TRADITIONAL GARLIC BREAD

There isn't really a set recipe for minestrone as it is usually made out of whatever vegetables are in season or left over in the fridge. The American food writer Angelo Pellegrini once said that the base of minestrone is bean broth, and that a genuine minestrone should use only Roman (borlotti) beans. While I agree that a minestrone has to contain some kind of pulse, I think the one you choose is really up to you. I have used cannellini beans here, but feel free to use borlotti if you prefer.

~~~~~~~~~~~~~~~~~~~~~~~~~~~~~~~~~

Serves 6

2 CARROTS, PEELED AND CUT INTO 5MM CUBES

3 CELERY STICKS, CUT INTO 5MM CUBES

1 BAKING POTATO, PEELED AND CUT INTO 1CM CUBES

2 ONIONS, PEELED AND ROUGHLY CHOPPED

6 TABLESPOONS EXTRA VIRGIN OLIVE OIL

2.5 LITRES VEGETABLE STOCK, MADE WITH 3 STOCK CUBES

2 COURGETTES, CUT INTO 5MM CUBES

1 X 400G TIN CANNELLINI BEANS, DRAINED

200G CONCHIGLIETTE (SMALL SHELL-SHAPED PASTA)

1 LARGE CIABATTA LOAF

2 GARLIC CLOVES, PEELED

3 TABLESPOONS FRESHLY CHOPPED FLAT LEAF PARSLEY

SALT AND BLACK PEPPER TO TASTE

Place the carrots, celery, potato and onions in a large saucepan. Add the oil and fry over a medium heat for 5 minutes until softened and starting to turn golden brown. Stir occasionally with a wooden spoon.

Pour in the stock. When it starts to boil, add the courgettes and beans, lower the heat and simmer for 15 minutes, stirring occasionally. Season with salt and pepper.

Add the pasta and continue to cook, uncovered, for about 6 minutes,

stirring occasionally and adding a little more hot water if necessary, until al dente..

Meanwhile, cut the ciabatta into slices 1cm thick and toast on both sides. Gently rub the garlic on one side of the toasted bread.

Once the pasta is cooked, take the pan off the heat, mix in the parsley and check the seasoning.

Divide the minestrone between 6 warm serving bowls and serve immediately, accompanied by the garlic bread.

ZUPPA DI FAGIOLI

TRADITIONAL NEAPOLITAN BEAN SOUP

If you are looking for a wholesome, old-fashioned soup, this is the one for you. Even people who don't like beans like this soup. Many people tend to assume that Italian bean soups will contain pasta, perhaps because of Pasta e Fagioli, which is a completely different dish, but I promise you, pasta in this instance just isn't needed. I absolutely love this soup, and although we didn't really eat it much in Italy, it still reminds me of home.

~~~~~~~~~~~~

Serves 6

4 TABLESPOONS OLIVE OIL

1 LARGE WHITE ONION, PEELED
  AND FINELY CHOPPED

150G DICED PANCETTA

2 TABLESPOONS FRESHLY CHOPPED
  ROSEMARY LEAVES

½ TEASPOON DRIED CHILLI FLAKES

1 X 400G TIN BORLOTTI BEANS,
  DRAINED

1 X 400G TIN CANNELLINI BEANS,
  DRAINED

1 X 400G TIN CHICKPEAS, DRAINED

1 X 400G TIN LENTILS, DRAINED

100G TINNED CHOPPED TOMATOES

1.5 LITRES VEGETABLE STOCK,
  MADE WITH 2 STOCK CUBES

2 TABLESPOONS FRESHLY CHOPPED
  FLAT LEAF PARSLEY

SALT TO TASTE

WARM CRUSTY BREAD TO SERVE

Place the oil in a large saucepan over a medium heat. Fry the onion and pancetta for 8 minutes, stirring occasionally, until the onion has softened.

Add the rosemary and chilli flakes, cook for a further 2 minutes, then add the beans, chickpeas and lentils. Stir well and cook for 3 minutes.

Add the tomatoes and stock and bring to a simmer. Cook on a low heat, uncovered, for 30 minutes, stirring occasionally.

Season with salt, fold in the parsley and allow to rest for 5 minutes. Serve in warm bowls with a few slices of warm crusty bread.

BRODO DI GALLINA

CLASSIC CHICKEN BROTH

I must dedicate this recipe to my mother-in-law, Elizabeth, because I first learnt the basic version from her back in 1995. Since then I have changed it to make it more personal to me – and, of course, more Italian. Whenever anyone in our family feels they are fighting a bug, I make them a bowl of this soup and – I don't know how or why – but they are fit and well the next day. It must be something in the water!

~~~~~~~~~~~~~~~~~~~~~~~~

Serves 8

1 BOILER CHICKEN, ABOUT 1.5KG, CUT INTO 6 PIECES

2 LEEKS, WASHED AND HALVED LENGTHWAYS

2 CELERY STICKS, HALVED

4 CARROTS, PEELED AND CUT INTO 3CM CHUNKS

1 PARSNIP, PEELED AND QUARTERED

3 LITRES VEGETABLE STOCK, MADE WITH 3 STOCK CUBES

350G ORZO (TINY PASTA SHAPED LIKE RICE)

3 EGGS

80G FRESHLY GRATED PARMESAN CHEESE

SALT AND WHITE PEPPER TO TASTE

Place the chicken, leeks, celery, carrots and parsnip in a large saucepan. Add the stock and bring to the boil, then turn down the heat and simmer for 1 hour. Using a large slotted spoon, transfer the chicken to a plate and leave to cool down.

Strain the broth into a medium-sized saucepan, discarding the vegetables. Season with salt and pepper and set aside.

Peel all the flesh off the chicken pieces, discarding the skin and bones, and place in the broth. Bring to a gentle boil. Add the pasta to the broth and cook until al dente.

Take the pan off the heat, crack in the eggs and sprinkle in the Parmesan. Stir vigorously with a wooden spoon for 30 seconds, allowing the eggs to become lightly scrambled. Serve immediately.

BRODO DI GALLINA

AMALFI

PASSATO DI PISELLI

CREAMY FRESH PEA AND BASIL SOUP

This truly has to be the ultimate pea soup. It looks fantastic, smells amazing and has a stunning taste. I normally stay away from creamy soups as starters, but this one is definitely an exception. Although filling, it's extremely light in texture. If you are stuck for fresh peas, you can use good-quality frozen ones, but always, always use fresh herbs – in this case basil. The soup is perfect served with focaccia bread on the side.

~~~~~~

Serves 4

2 TABLESPOONS SALTED BUTTER
6 SHALLOTS, PEELED AND FINELY
 CHOPPED
500G FRESH PEAS, PODDED WEIGHT
 (OR 500G FROZEN)
500ML VEGETABLE STOCK, MADE
 WITH A STOCK CUBE

10 FRESH BASIL LEAVES
100ML DOUBLE CREAM, PLUS A LITTLE
 EXTRA TO SERVE
SALT AND WHITE PEPPER TO TASTE

Melt the butter in a large saucepan over a medium heat and fry the shallots for 2 minutes, stirring occasionally with a wooden spoon.

Add the peas and cook for 3 minutes, stirring constantly. Pour in the stock, add the basil and bring to the boil. Lower the heat and simmer for 25 minutes. Stir occasionally.

Take the saucepan off the heat and use a hand blender to blitz the contents into a smooth creamy soup. Pour in the cream, season with salt and pepper and reheat without boiling.

Serve in warmed bowls, topped with a drizzle of cream.

ZUPPA DI PESCE

MY GRANDFATHER'S SPECIAL SPICY FISH SOUP

Every time I make fish soup, I can't believe how something so tasty and good for you can be so easy to prepare. If fish isn't a must-have in your house, try to make this dish for your family every now and then. I am a strong believer that we should all eat more fish – it is such a great source of protein and has some excellent natural oils. If you wish, plaice or cod can be used instead of haddock.

~~~~~~~~~~~~~~~~~

Serves 6

24 LARGE RAW UNSHELLED PRAWNS

600ML FISH STOCK

3 TABLESPOONS EXTRA VIRGIN
   OLIVE OIL

1 LARGE RED ONION, PEELED AND
   FINELY CHOPPED

1 TEASPOON DRIED CHILLI FLAKES

200G ROASTED MIXED PEPPERS
   IN BRINE, DRAINED AND SLICED

200ML WHITE WINE

1 X 400G TIN CHOPPED TOMATOES

100G FROZEN PEAS, DEFROSTED

400G HADDOCK, SKINNED AND CUT
   INTO 3CM CHUNKS

400G RED MULLET OR SEA BASS,
   SKINNED AND CUT INTO 3CM
   CHUNKS

4 TABLESPOONS FRESHLY CHOPPED
   FLAT LEAF PARSLEY

SALT TO TASTE

Shell the prawns, but leave the tails on. Put the shells and fish stock in a saucepan and bring to the boil. (The shells give terrific flavour.) Lower the heat and simmer for 10 minutes. Strain, discarding the shells, and set aside.

Place the oil in a large saucepan over a medium heat and fry the onion, chilli and peppers for 5 minutes, stirring occasionally. Pour in the wine and cook for a further 3 minutes so the alcohol evaporates. Add the stock, tomatoes and peas. Season with salt, bring to the boil and cook, uncovered, over a medium heat for 20 minutes.

Add the fish and prawns, stir well and cook for a further 10 minutes. Stir in the parsley, check the seasoning.

Serve immediately. Buon appetito!

ZUPPA DI ZUCCA E PATATE

ZUPPA DI ZUCCA E PATATE

Potato and Butternut Squash Soup

My wife often makes this soup, either as a main meal or a starter, and we all love it. She used to cook it with butter and cream but I proved to her that my recipe is much lower in calories and fat, yet has exactly the same taste. Nowadays she will only cook it Gino's way. You can use pumpkin instead of butternut squash if you prefer, and can create a thicker soup by adding slightly less stock.

~~~~~~~~~~~~~~~~~~~~~~~~~~~~~~

Serves 6

3 TABLESPOONS EXTRA VIRGIN
OLIVE OIL, PLUS EXTRA TO SERVE
1 WHITE ONION, PEELED AND
ROUGHLY CHOPPED
1 MEDIUM BUTTERNUT SQUASH

1 LARGE FLOURY POTATO, PEELED
AND QUARTERED
1.2 LITRES VEGETABLE STOCK
300ML FULL-FAT MILK
SALT AND WHITE PEPPER TO TASTE
150G ROCKET LEAVES TO GARNISH

Place the oil in a large saucepan over a medium heat and fry the onion for 3 minutes until soft, stirring occasionally with a wooden spoon.

Meanwhile, use a sharp knife to peel the butternut squash. Scoop out and discard the seeds, then cut the flesh into 3cm chunks.

Add the squash and potato quarters to the saucepan and fry for 3 minutes until starting to soften.

Pour in the stock, bring to the boil, then lower the heat and cook very gently, uncovered, for 20 minutes. Stir occasionally.

Pour in the milk and cook for a further 20 minutes, then use a hand blender to blitz into a smooth creamy soup. Season with salt and pepper.

Serve hot, garnished with the rocket leaves and a drizzle of extra virgin olive oil on top.

PASTA

* * * * * * * * * * * * * * *

IT WOULD BE NEARLY IMPOSSIBLE FOR ME to write any book, without having a few pasta dish options. When I was growing up, pasta was eaten nearly every day, and it is still a must-have in our family. I eat pasta at least four times a week. An Italian without pasta is like a Brit without fish and chips – it's just impossible to picture.

In Italy at the moment we have more than 650 different shapes of pasta. Each pasta shape and size was created for a particular sauce, and most Italians stick by those rules, but pasta is now so popular worldwide that many dishes have been adapted. For example, spaghetti bolognese doesn't exist to us Italians – whenever we make a meat sauce, we use either tagliatelle or pappardelle.

Traditionally, pasta is made from an unleavened dough of a durum wheat flour mixed with water, then formed into sheets or various shapes. It can also be made with eggs instead of water, so is divided into two categories: dried (pasta secca) and fresh (pasta fresca).

Fresh pasta is, more often than not, locally made with fresh ingredients – usually a mixture of eggs and plain flour or 'OO' high-gluten flour. As it contains eggs, it's much softer than dried pasta and takes only about half the time to cook. (Also, it doesn't expand in size after cooking.) Fresh egg pasta is generally cut into strands of various widths and thicknesses, depending on the type to be made (e.g. fettuccine, pappardelle and lasagne), and is generally best with delicate sauces that will allow the pasta to take centre stage.

The ingredients required to make dried pasta include semolina flour and water. Unlike fresh pasta, dried pasta needs to be dried at a low temperature for several days to evaporate all the moisture, which means that it can be stored for longer periods than its fresh counterpart.

Pasta manufacture is big business. It is estimated that Italians eat over 26kg of pasta per person per year. In fact, it is so loved that individual consumption exceeds the country's average wheat production, so Italy frequently has to import wheat for pasta-making. Although pasta is now produced everywhere, the Italian products stick to time-tested production methods that create a superior pasta, which means that many people still buy only Italian-produced pasta.

Gragnano is the home of pasta in southern Italy. Yes, it's true that every region has its favourite local pasta shape but in Gragnano there is an entire street of independent pasta factories and shops, each making its own traditional shapes as well as the most commonly known ones. Tiny factories, like the one I visited there, produce vast quantities every day. The factories are humid but huge fans air-dry the pasta after it has been made.

* * * * * * * * * * * * * * *

Some are shaped by hand and others by machine but there's always true passion and commitment in the way it's made.

Once the pasta has dried, it is weighed and packed by hand into the factories' signature packets. Buyers can test and view the products in showrooms alongside the factories, and it's lovely to see the doors constantly swing open with *nonnas* (grannies) coming in with their shopping trolleys to buy enough pasta to feed a small army.

There are several health benefits to eating pasta, especially wholewheat pasta, which is low in calories and high in vitamins, minerals and complex carbohydrates: it releases energy slowly compared to sugar, providing energy for a longer time. And, contrary to popular belief, it's not fattening, unless it's combined with rich fatty sauces. Italians are one of the thinnest and healthiest nations in the world, and most of them eat pasta daily!

I absolutely believe that pasta is the ultimate fast food dish – so much so that I am willing to put my money where my mouth is and you will see many 'Gino's Pasta Bars' on your high streets soon. It's quick, easy to prepare, healthy, filling and, most importantly, delicious. Children love it – in fact, who doesn't like a plate of pasta?

If none of the above has convinced you, I hope the recipes I have chosen will get you tempted. In this chapter, you will find a collection of tasty, stylish yet very simple pasta dishes, which can be used as a starter, quick meal or dinner. I've also chosen ingredients that are very widely available so that you won't be driven mad trying to find them. I hope you enjoy these dishes; I'm confident they will become regulars in your weekly menu as they are in mine!

GINO'S GOLDEN RULES FOR PASTA

* Make sure your saucepan is large enough – one that's 24cm in diameter and at least 18cm tall is ideal.

* For that perfect al dente bite, cook the pasta for 1 minute less than specified on the packet.

* Make sure the water is boiling before you add the pasta, and never add oil to it – contrary to popular belief, it won't stop the pasta sticking together!

* Ensure you have enough water in the pan. You will need 4.5 litres for every 500g of pasta.

* Always cook pasta in salted water with the lid off.

* Toss the cooked pasta in your chosen sauce rather than simply placing the sauce on top.

HOME-MADE EGG PASTA DOUGH

Making your own pasta is really satisfying, and if you are making it for a special evening, your guests will be hugely impressed. It really isn't as hard as you would imagine, so please try it – the flavour is so good. This recipe is for a simple pasta dough that can be used to make lasagne sheets, fettuccine or pappardelle. Make sure your eggs are at room temperature – it really helps with the combining.

~~~~~~~~~~~~~~~~~~~~~~~~~~~~~~~~~~

Makes about 500g dough

400G WHITE FLOUR, TYPE 'OO'
3 EGGS
2 EGG YOLKS

½ TEASPOON FINE SALT
2 TABLESPOONS EXTRA VIRGIN OLIVE OIL

Sift the flour into a large bowl. Make a well in the centre and break in the whole eggs. Add the egg yolks, salt and oil, then stir with the handle of a wooden spoon until the mixture has a crumbly texture. Tip onto a well-floured work surface and knead until you have a soft dough.

Once the dough has come together, continue to knead for about 10 minutes, using both hands, as if kneading bread.

Roll the dough into a ball, cover with cling film and leave to rest in the fridge for 30 minutes. This will allow the dough to become more elastic and easier to use.

When the dough has rested, unwrap it and flatten with your fingers so that it can fit through the rollers of a pasta machine.

Flour the dough lightly on both sides and pass it through the machine several times, from the widest setting to the thinnest. Make sure you keep the pasta dusted with flour at all times.

If you don't have a pasta machine, roll the pasta by hand with a rolling pin on a lightly floured surface until it is 2mm thick.

FRESH EGG FETTUCCINE

This is a simple way to make and cut your own fettucine by hand, using the pasta dough recipe opposite. If you have children, I really recommend making this with them – they will love it. The last time my boys and I made fresh egg fettuccine together, they decided to hang the pasta ribbons over a broom handle across two chairs as this is how my grandmother used to do it. A less messy alternative is to hang the ribbons from a coat hanger suspended over a tray.

Makes about 500g

1 QUANTITY HOME-MADE EGG PASTA DOUGH (SEE OPPOSITE)   **PLAIN FLOUR FOR DUSTING**

Place the rested dough on a floured work surface and flatten it with the palm of your hand. Dust the rolling pin with flour, then roll it across the dough towards the centre. Continue rolling backwards and forwards, turning the dough every so often, until evenly flattened and you can see your fingers through it.

Fold one edge of the pasta sheet to the centre, then fold the opposite edge in the same way. You should end up with a flattened cigar shape.

Flour the pasta well, then use a long sharp knife to cut it into widthways strips 5mm wide. Slide the flat of the knife lengthways under the pasta along the join, then gently lift it up and the strips will fall open and hang down on either side of the blade.

If you are cooking the pasta immediately, lightly dust the strips with flour and cook within the hour. If you want to save the strips for future use, transfer them to a hanger and allow them to dry.

RIGATONI ALL' ARRABBIATA CON SALMONE

RIGATONI IN SPICY TOMATO AND SALMON SAUCE

Arrabbiata means 'angry' in Italian, and I guess they used it to name this dish because of the heat of the chilli peppers in the sauce. The spicier the better for me, but be careful in Italy when asking for this traditional dish to be extra spicy – they will take you at your word. In this recipe the rigatoni can be replaced with penne or any other pasta shape, if you prefer. Just get cooking – it's delicious.

~~~~~~~~~~

Serves 4

6 TABLESPOONS EXTRA VIRGIN OLIVE OIL

2 GARLIC CLOVES, PEELED AND FINELY SLICED

2 MEDIUM-HOT RED CHILLIES, DESEEDED AND FINELY SLICED

2 X 400G TINS OF CHOPPED TOMATOES

3 TABLESPOONS FRESHLY CHOPPED FLAT LEAF PARSLEY

400G SALMON FILLET, CUT INTO 1CM CUBES

500G RIGATONI

SALT TO TASTE

Heat the oil in a large frying pan or wok over a medium heat and stir-fry the garlic and chillies with a wooden spoon for about 1 minute until sizzling.

Add the tomatoes and parsley, stir well and simmer gently, uncovered, for 10 minutes, stirring every couple of minutes.

Carefully stir in the salmon and season with salt. Remove from the heat and set to one side.

Meanwhile, cook the pasta in a large pan of boiling, salted water until al dente. Drain well and tip it back into the same pan.

Place the pan over a low heat, pour in the sauce and stir for 30 seconds to allow the flavours to combine properly. Serve immediately.

RIGATONI ALL' ARRABBIATA CON SALMONE

TORRE DEL GRECO

CANNELLONI AL PESTO GENOVESE

ROLLED FILLED PASTA WITH PESTO AND BÉCHAMEL SAUCE

Cannelloni was invented in Sorrento in the early 1900s by
a chef from Naples. Today you'll find a recipe for it in many
Italian cookery books, so I had to include a version here. As
you'll see, this is a traditional-style cannelloni with a bit of
a twist, and I think you will love the result.

~~~~~~~~~~~~~~~~~~~~~~~~~~~~~~~

Serves 4

4 TABLESPOONS OLIVE OIL

1 LARGE ONION, PEELED AND FINELY
   CHOPPED

1 CARROT, PEELED AND FINELY
   CHOPPED

1 COURGETTE, FINELY CHOPPED

500G MINCED BEEF

½ GLASS OF RED WINE

1 TABLESPOON TOMATO PURÉE

5 FRESH BASIL LEAVES

350ML PASSATA (SIEVED TOMATOES)

12 READY-MADE FRESH PASTA SHEETS

SALT AND PEPPER TO TASTE

For the pesto

30G PINE NUTS

100G FRESH BASIL LEAVES

1 GARLIC CLOVE, PEELED

170ML EXTRA VIRGIN OLIVE OIL

30G FRESHLY GRATED PARMESAN
   CHEESE

For the béchamel sauce

50G BUTTER

50G PLAIN FLOUR

500ML SEMI-SKIMMED MILK

50G FRESHLY GRATED PARMESAN
   CHEESE

Place the oil in a large saucepan over a low heat and gently fry the onion,
carrot and courgette for 10 minutes, until softened.

Add the minced beef and stir continuously for a further 5 minutes to allow
the meat to cook evenly. Add the wine, bring to a simmer and cook gently
for a couple of minutes to allow the alcohol to evaporate.

Add the tomato purée, basil leaves and passata, stirring with a wooden
spoon. Simmer on a low heat, with the lid half on, for 30 minutes, stirring
occasionally. Season with salt and pepper, then leave to cool at room
temperature.

CANNELLONI AL PESTO GENOVESE

To make the pesto, put the pine nuts, basil, garlic, olive oil and Parmesan in a food processor or blender and blitz together. Set aside.

Preheat the oven to 180°C/gas mark 4.

To make the béchamel sauce, melt the butter in a large saucepan over a low heat. Add the flour, whisking constantly, until you get a thick, creamy texture with a light brown colour. Pour in a third of the milk and continue whisking. When the mixture starts to thicken, pour in another third of the milk and continue whisking. Once thickened again, pour in the rest of the milk and the Parmesan. Whisk until the sauce has a custard-like consistency. Remove from the heat and mix in the prepared pesto.

Pour a third of the pesto béchamel into the bottom of a baking dish measuring about 30 x 20cm and 5cm deep.

Place a pasta sheet on a chopping board with the longer side nearest you and put a heaped tablespoon of the beef sauce along one edge. Gently roll the pasta forward to create a filled cannelloni. Repeat until all the pasta sheets are filled. Place the cannelloni, seam downwards, in the baking dish and pour the remaining pesto béchamel over them.

Bake in the oven for 45 minutes until the top is golden brown and crispy. Set aside to rest for 10 minutes before serving – this helps the cannelloni to hold together better.

If you are preparing the cannelloni the day before you plan to eat it, cover with cling film and refrigerate. Take out of the fridge 20 minutes before cooking, and bake in a preheated oven at 180°C/gas mark 4 for 45 minutes.

FETTUCCINE ALLA BOLOGNESE

FETTUCCINE ALLA BOLOGNESE

FETTUCCINE WITH A SUCCULENT MEAT AND RED WINE SAUCE

There is nothing better than coming home after a long day's work and enjoying a huge plate of fettuccine alla bolognese. It's like getting a warm hug. You can use pappardelle here if you prefer, but never use spaghetti – it simply doesn't work because you need a flat surface for the sauce to cling to.

Serves 6

6 TABLESPOONS OLIVE OIL

1 WHITE ONION, PEELED AND
   FINELY CHOPPED

250G DICED PANCETTA

1 LARGE CARROT, PEELED AND
   FINELY GRATED

2 CELERY STICKS, FINELY CHOPPED

400G MINCED BEEF

400G MINCED PORK

150ML DRY RED WINE

2 X 400G TINS CHOPPED TOMATOES

3 TABLESPOONS TOMATO PURÉE

10 FRESH BASIL LEAVES

200ML BEEF STOCK

500G FRESH EGG FETTUCCINE

100G FRESHLY GRATED PECORINO OR
   PARMESAN CHEESE

SALT AND BLACK PEPPER TO TASTE

Place the olive oil in a large saucepan over a medium heat and fry the onion, pancetta, carrot and celery for 8 minutes until softened, stirring occasionally with a wooden spoon.

Add the minced beef and pork and cook for a further 5 minutes, stirring continuously until coloured all over. Season with salt and pepper. Add the wine and cook for 5 more minutes until the alcohol has evaporated.

Add the tomatoes, tomato purée, basil and stock, lower the heat and cook, uncovered, for 2 hours, stirring every 20 minutes or so, until you have a beautiful rich sauce. When ready, season and set aside.

Meanwhile, cook the pasta in a large pan of boiling, salted water until al dente. Drain and return to the pan. Add the meat sauce and stir gently over a low heat for 30 seconds. Serve with Pecorino sprinkled on top.

SPAGHETTI ALLA CARBONARA

SPAGHETTI ALLA CARBONARA

SPAGHETTI WITH EGGS, PANCETTA AND PECORINO ROMANO

Carbonara is the Italian word for 'charcoal burner', so some people believe this dish was first made for charcoal workers in the Apennine mountains. The general view now, though, is that it was an urban dish invented in Rome. Note that cream is not used in an authentic *carbonara*, so none is included below. Fettuccine or bucatini can be substituted for the more usual spaghetti.

~~~~~~~~~~~~~~~~~~~~~

Serves 4

5 TABLESPOONS EXTRA VIRGIN OLIVE OIL	6 TABLESPOONS FRESHLY GRATED PECORINO CHEESE
3 TABLESPOONS UNSALTED BUTTER	4 TABLESPOONS FINELY CHOPPED FLAT-LEAF PARSLEY
250G DICED PANCETTA	500G SPAGHETTI
4 EGGS	SALT AND BLACK PEPPER TO TASTE

Heat the oil and butter in large frying pan over a medium heat and fry the pancetta for 8 minutes, stirring occasionally, until golden and crispy. Set aside.

Whisk the eggs and half the cheese in a bowl. Add the parsley and plenty of black pepper. Set aside.

Cook the spaghetti in a large pan of boiling, salted water until al dente. Drain well and tip it back into the same pan.

Tip the contents of the pancetta pan into the pasta, then pour in the egg mixture. Mix everything together for 30 seconds with a wooden spoon. The heat from the pasta will be sufficient to cook the egg to a creamy coating.

Season with salt and pepper and serve immediately with the remaining cheese sprinkled on top.

ORECCHIETTE CON CIME DI RAPE

ORECCHIETTE WITH BROCCOLI, GARLIC AND CHILLI

I grew up eating orecchiette, the typical pasta shape of Puglia. The name translates as 'little ears', which is exactly what the shape resembles. Italian grandmothers traditionally make the pasta by hand, shaping it while having a good old chat. The hollow in the little ears perfectly entraps whatever sauce they are served with.

~~~~~~

Serves 4

6 TABLESPOONS OLIVE OIL

1 GARLIC CLOVE, PEELED AND
  FINELY CHOPPED

1 SMALL RED CHILLI, DESEEDED
  AND FINELY CHOPPED

6 SMALL CHERRY TOMATOES,
  QUARTERED

2 TABLESPOONS FINELY CHOPPED
  FRESH PARSLEY

500G ORECCHIETTE

200G BROCCOLI FLORETS

SALT AND BLACK PEPPER TO TASTE

40G FRESHLY GRATED PECORINO
  CHEESE TO GARNISH (OPTIONAL)

Heat the olive oil in a pan over a medium heat. Add the garlic, chilli and tomatoes and fry for 2–3 minutes until the tomatoes are softened. Stir in the parsley.

Meanwhile, cook the pasta in a large pan of boiling salted water until 1 minute away from being al dente. At that point, add the broccoli florets and cook for 1 minute. Drain the mixture and add it to the sauce. Mix well and season to taste.

Pile the pasta into serving bowls or deep plates, and grate some Pecorino over it, if desired.

ORECCHIETTE CON CIME DI RAPE

GNOCCHI ALLA SORRENTINA

POTATO DUMPLINGS WITH TOMATO AND MOZZARELLA SAUCE

Good gnocchi should be light, like little clouds, cetainly not heavy. If you don't have the time to make them from scratch and are buying them from a supermarket, look for ones that are at least 70 per cent potato as this means they are good quality. Those with a lower percentage are full of flour.

~~~~~~~~~~~~~~~~~~~

Serves 4

4 TABLESPOONS OLIVE OIL

1 LARGE WHITE ONION, PEELED AND FINELY CHOPPED

2 X 400G TINS CHOPPED TOMATOES

10 FRESH BASIL LEAVES, PLUS EXTRA FOR GARNISH

600G FLOURY POTATOES, UNPEELED

2 EGGS, LIGHTLY BEATEN

1 EGG YOLK

200G PLAIN FLOUR, PLUS EXTRA FOR DUSTING

2 MOZZARELLA BALLS, DRAINED AND CUT INTO SMALL CUBES

SALT AND BLACK PEPPER TO TASTE

50G FRESHLY GRATED PARMESAN CHEESE TO SERVE

Heat the oil in a large saucepan over a medium heat and fry the onion for 5 minutes, stirring occasionally with a wooden spoon, until soft.

Add the chopped tomatoes and basil, stir well and bring to a simmer. Cook gently, uncovered, for 10 minutes, stirring every couple of minutes. Once ready, season with salt and pepper and set aside.

Cook the whole potatoes in a large saucepan of boiling water for 25–30 minutes until tender. Drain well and cool slightly.

Peel the potatoes and press the flesh through a potato ricer into a large bowl. While it is still warm, add 2 pinches of salt, all the eggs and the flour. Lightly mix, then turn out onto a floured surface. Knead lightly until you have soft, slightly sticky dough. (Do not overwork it or the gnocchi will be tough).

GNOCCHI ALLA SORRENTINA

Meanwhile, cut the dough in half and roll each piece into a long sausage shape about 1.5cm in diameter. Cut into 2cm pieces, then lay them out on a lightly floured clean tea towel.

Cook the gnocchi in a large pan of boiling salted water for 2 minutes. They are ready when they float to the surface. Using a slotted spoon, transfer them to the pan of tomato sauce.

Place the pan over a medium heat, add the mozzarella and stir gently for 30 seconds until slightly melted and the sauce is heated through.

Serve the gnocchi immediately, with Parmesan cheese sprinkled on top and a few basil leaves for garnish.

PAPPARDELLE CON POLPETTE

Pappardelle with Meatballs

This is a family favourite and a staple for the kids. True Italians would never serve spaghetti with meatballs; it has to be fettuccine or pappardelle pasta to be authentic.

~~~~~~~~~~~~~~~~~~~~~~~~~~~~~~~~~~~~~~

Serves 4

250G MINCED BEEF

1 EGG

HANDFUL OF FINELY CHOPPED FRESH
   FLAT LEAF PARSLEY

100G WHITE FLOUR, TYPE 'OO'

90ML OLIVE OIL

1 ONION, PEELED AND FINELY SLICED

1 RED CHILLI, DESEEDED AND FINELY
   SLICED

SMALL GLASS OF RED WINE

600G TINNED CHOPPED TOMATOES

500G PAPPARDELLE

SALT TO TASTE

100G FRESHLY GRATED PECORINO
   CHEESE TO GARNISH

In a large bowl, mix the minced beef, egg and parsley together. Season to taste.

Take a teaspoonful of the meat mixture and use your hands to roll it into a ball. Dust the ball in the flour and put to one side. Repeat with the rest of the mixture.

Heat the olive oil in a frying pan and gently sauté the onion and chilli until soft. Add the meatballs and fry gently for about 6 minutes until golden brown. Now add the wine and simmer for about 2 minutes until the alcohol has evaporated. Add the chopped tomatoes, season to taste and cook for a further 4 minutes.

Meanwhile, cook the pappardelle in a large pan of boiling, salted water until al dente. Drain and add it to the sauce. Mix well.

Serve the pasta topped with the freshly grated Pecorino cheese.

AMALFI

FETTUCCINE CON POLLO E GORGONZOLA

Fresh Pasta with Chicken and Gorgonzola Sauce

If you enjoy a chicken pasta bake, this is the dish for you. Adding wine, chives and gutsy Gorgonzola piccante cheese gives the meat an amazing flavour and makes for a really hearty and satisfying meal. The Gorgonzola can be replaced with milder Dolcelatte if you prefer.

~~~~~~~~~~~~~~~~

Serves 4

3 TABLESPOONS OLIVE OIL

300G BONELESS AND SKINLESS CHICKEN BREAST, CUT INTO THIN STRIPS

100ML DRY WHITE WINE

300ML DOUBLE CREAM

250G GORGONZOLA PICCANTE CHEESE, CUT INTO CHUNKS

3 TABLESPOONS FRESHLY CHOPPED CHIVES

500G FETTUCCINE (SEE PAGE 69)

SALT AND BLACK PEPPER TO TASTE

Heat the oil in a saucepan over a medium heat and fry the chicken for 6 minutes, stirring occasionally, until golden all over.

Pour in the wine and heat for 2 minutes so that the alcohol evaporates. Add the cream and Gorgonzola and cook for a further 3 minutes, stirring continuously.

Mix in the chives and season with salt and plenty of black pepper, then set aside.

Cook the fettuccine in a large pan of boiling, salted water until al dente. Drain well and tip it back into the same pan.

Pour the creamy chicken sauce over the pasta and stir off the heat for 30 seconds so that the sauce coats it beautifully.

Serve immediately with more black pepper sprinkled on top.

FETTUCCINE CON POLLO E GORGONZOLA

RAVIOLI CON SALMONE E RICOTTA

RAVIOLI CON SALMONE E RICOTTA

RAVIOLI FILLED WITH SMOKED SALMON AND RICOTTA

When I was a child, eating smoked salmon was always a massive treat because it was so expensive. It's cheaper now, but still fantastic. Just take care when seasoning the dish because the salmon is already salty.

~~~~~~~~~~~~~~~~~~~~~~~

Serves 6

**1 QUANTITY HOME-MADE EGG PASTA
DOUGH (SEE PAGE 68)**
2 EGGS, BEATEN
100ML EXTRA VIRGIN OLIVE OIL
SMOKED PAPRIKA
SALT AND BLACK PEPPER TO TASTE

For the filling
500G RICOTTA CHEESE
ZEST OF 2 UNWAXED LEMONS
**300G SMOKED SALMON, FINELY
CHOPPED**
**3 TABLESPOONS FINELY CHOPPED
FRESH CHIVES**

First make the filling. Place all the ingredients in a large bowl and mix together with a fork. Season with salt and pepper. Cover with cling film and refrigerate for 10 minutes.

Flatten the dough so that it can fit through the rollers of a pasta machine. Flour lightly on both sides and pass it through the machine several times, from the widest setting to the thinnest. Keep it floured at all times. If you don't have a pasta machine, roll the pasta by hand with a rolling pin on a lightly floured surface until it is 2mm thick.

Lay the pasta sheet on a well-floured surface. Put teaspoonfuls of filling at 4cm intervals across half of it. Brush the spaces between the filling with the beaten egg. Fold the empty half of the dough over the top and press down between the mounds of filling to make self-contained parcels. Use a pastry wheel or knife to cut between the parcels, leaving a 5mm border around each one.

Cook the ravioli in a large pan of salted water for 3 minutes (doing them in batches if necessary). Drain and place on a large serving plate. Season with a little salt and pepper, drizzle over the oil and sprinkle with paprika.

LINGUINE AI FRUTTI DI MARE

LINGUINE WITH SPICY SEAFOOD SAUCE

It's very important to use tinned cherry tomatoes in the sauce for this dish because fresh ones make it too watery.

~~~~~~

Serves 4

200G CLAMS

200G MUSSELS

150ML DRY WHITE WINE

6 TABLESPOONS EXTRA VIRGIN OLIVE
  OIL

4 GARLIC CLOVES, PEELED AND SLICED

½ TEASPOON DRIED CHILLI FLAKES

2 X 400G TINS CHERRY TOMATOES

200G BABY SQUID, CUT INTO RINGS

200G PEELED RAW PRAWNS

4 TABLESPOONS FRESHLY CHOPPED
  FLAT LEAF PARSLEY

500G LINGUINE

ZEST OF 1 UNWAXED LEMON

SALT AND BLACK PEPPER TO TASTE

Wash the clams and mussels in cold water. Discard any that have cracked shells or that do not close when tapped firmly. Place in a large saucepan, add the wine and cook, covered, over a medium heat for 3 minutes until the shells have opened. Discard any that remain closed. Tip into a colander placed over a bowl and set aside.

Pour the oil into the empty saucepan and gently fry the garlic for about a minute until it begins to sizzle. Add the chilli flakes and tomatoes and cook over a medium heat, stirring occasionally, for 5 minutes. Season with salt.

Pour 6 tablespoons of the shellfish liquor into the sauce and continue to simmer for 2 minutes. Stir in the squid and prawns and cook for a further 3 minutes until both are pink. Add the clams, mussels and parsley and stir until combined and heated through.

Meanwhile, cook the linguine in a large pan of boiling salted water until al dente. Drain and add the pasta to the sauce.

Sprinkle the lemon zest all over and mix on a low heat for 30 seconds until the pasta is evenly coated and heated through. Serve immediately.

LINGUINE AI FRUTTI DI MARE

LASAGNE DI MAMMA

MY MOTHER'S LASAGNE

This recipe has been handed down in the D'Acampo family for many generations, though I call it 'Lasagne di Mamma' because my mother taught it to my sister and me when we were about 11 years old. It's a great tradition that my wife will pass on to our own children. Allowing the dish to rest for a good 10 minutes before serving allows the layers to firm up slightly and become easier to cut neatly.

~~~~~~~~~~~~~~~~

Serves 6–8

12 FRESH LASAGNE SHEETS, EACH ABOUT 10 X 18CM

50G FRESHLY GRATED PARMESAN CHEESE

50G COLD SALTED BUTTER, CUT INTO 1CM CUBES

SALT AND PEPPER TO TASTE

For the béchamel sauce

100G SALTED BUTTER

100G PLAIN FLOUR

1 LITRE COLD FULL-FAT MILK

50G FRESHLY GRATED PARMESAN CHEESE

¼ FRESHLY GRATED NUTMEG

For the meat sauce

5 TABLESPOONS OLIVE OIL

1 ONION, PEELED AND FINELY CHOPPED

1 LARGE CARROT, PEELED AND GRATED

1 CELERY STICK, FINELY CHOPPED

500G MINCED BEEF OR LAMB

2 GLASSES OF ITALIAN DRY RED WINE

1 X 700ML BOTTLE PASSATA (SIEVED TOMATOES)

1 TABLESPOON TOMATO PURÉE

10 FRESH BASIL LEAVES

First make the meat sauce. Heat the olive oil in a large saucepan over a medium heat and fry the onion, carrot and celery for 5 minutes, stirring occasionally with a wooden spoon.

Add the minced beef and continue to cook for a further 5 minutes, stirring constantly, until coloured all over. Season with salt and pepper and cook for 5 more minutes.

LASAGNE DI MAMMA

TORRE DEL GRECO

Pour in the wine, stir well and cook for 5 minutes until the alcohol has evaporated.

Add the passata, tomato purée and basil, then lower the heat and cook, uncovered, for 1 hour, stirring occasionally, until you get a beautiful rich sauce. Taste and season after about 30 minutes.

Preheat the oven to 180°C/gas mark 4.

Meanwhile, to make the béchamel sauce, melt the butter in a large saucepan over a medium heat. Stir in the flour and cook for 1 minute until it becomes light brown in colour. Gradually whisk in the milk, lower the heat and cook for 10 minutes, whisking constantly. Once thickened, stir in the Parmesan and nutmeg. Season with salt and pepper and set aside to slightly cool.

Spread a quarter of the béchamel sauce in the bottom of a deep ovenproof dish measuring about 30 x 25cm. Lay 4 lasagne sheets on top and, if necessary, cut them to fit the dish.

Spread half the meat sauce over the pasta, then top with a third of the remaining béchamel sauce.

Lay 4 more sheets of lasagne on top and cover with the remaining meat sauce. Spread half the remaining béchamel sauce on top.

Arrange a final layer of lasagne sheets over the sauces, then gently spread the rest of the béchamel on top, making sure that you completely cover the pasta.

Sprinkle with the Parmesan and cubed butter. Finally, grind some black pepper over the top.

Cook in the bottom of the oven for 30 minutes, then place the dish in the middle of the oven, raise the temperature to 200°C/gas mark 6 and cook for a further 15 minutes until golden and crispy all over.

Set the dish aside to rest for 10 minutes before serving.

SPAGHETTI ALLA CALABRESE
Spaghetti with Anchovies, Breadcrumbs and Garlic

According to local legend, Calabrian girls were at one time obliged to master the preparation of 13 pasta dishes before they were able to marry. This recipe was one of them, and I totally understand why it was chosen. You can make the sauce even richer by including a few chopped olives and capers lightly cooked in oil. Either way, it's *fantastico*!

~~~~~~~~~~~~~~~~~~

Serves 4

8 TABLESPOONS EXTRA VIRGIN
  OLIVE OIL
4 GARLIC CLOVES, PEELED AND
  HALVED
2 MEDIUM-HOT RED CHILLIES,
  DESEEDED AND CHOPPED

8 PRESERVED ANCHOVY FILLETS,
  CHOPPED AND OIL RESERVED
100G FRESH WHITE BREADCRUMBS
500G SPAGHETTI
3 TABLESPOONS FRESHLY CHOPPED
  FLAT LEAF PARSLEY
SALT TO TASTE

Heat the oil in a pan over a low heat and gently fry the garlic for about a minute until golden all over. Transfer the garlic to a plate, then add the chillies and anchovies to the pan. Cook for about 3 minutes, stirring constantly, until the anchovies have melted. Set aside.

Add a little oil to a separate frying pan and toast the breadcrumbs for a couple of minutes until crispy and golden brown. Set aside.

Meanwhile, cook the pasta in a large pan of boiling, salted water until al dente. Drain well, then tip it back into the same pan.

Place the pan over a low heat. Add the reserved anchovy oil, the parsley and breadcrumbs and stir everything together for 30 seconds so the flavours combine properly.

Check if the pasta needs a little salt and serve immediately.

LINGUINE ALLE VONGOLE

Pasta with Clams, Garlic and Chilli

This is first meal I order whenever I go home to Naples. I absolutely love the flavour of fresh clams – so much so that I often order them just cooked in olive oil and garlic. You can replace the linguine with spaghetti if you prefer, but never put grated cheese on top – it doesn't work with the freshness of the sauce.

~~~~~~~~~~~~~~~~~~~~

Serves 4

700G CLAMS, CLEANED

150ML WHITE WINE

6 TABLESPOONS EXTRA VIRGIN
   OLIVE OIL

2 GARLIC CLOVES, PEELED AND SLICED

½ TEASPOON DRIED CHILLI FLAKES

10 CHERRY TOMATOES, HALVED

4 TABLESPOONS FRESHLY CHOPPED
   FLAT LEAF PARSLEY

500G LINGUINE

SALT TO TASTE

Wash the clams under cold water. Discard any that have cracked shells or that do not close when tapped firmly. Place them in a large saucepan with the wine, cover and cook over a medium heat for 4 minutes, until they have opened. Discard any that remain closed. Tip into a colander placed over a bowl and set aside.

Pour the oil into the empty saucepan and gently fry the garlic for about a minute until it begins to sizzle. Add the chilli, tomatoes and parsley and pour in the clam liquid from the bowl. Cook over a medium heat for 3 minutes. Season with salt.

Meanwhile, cook the pasta in a large pan of boiling, salted water until al dente. Drain and add it to the pan with the sauce and the clams. Gently mix everything together on a low heat for 30 seconds so the pasta is evenly coated. Serve immediately.

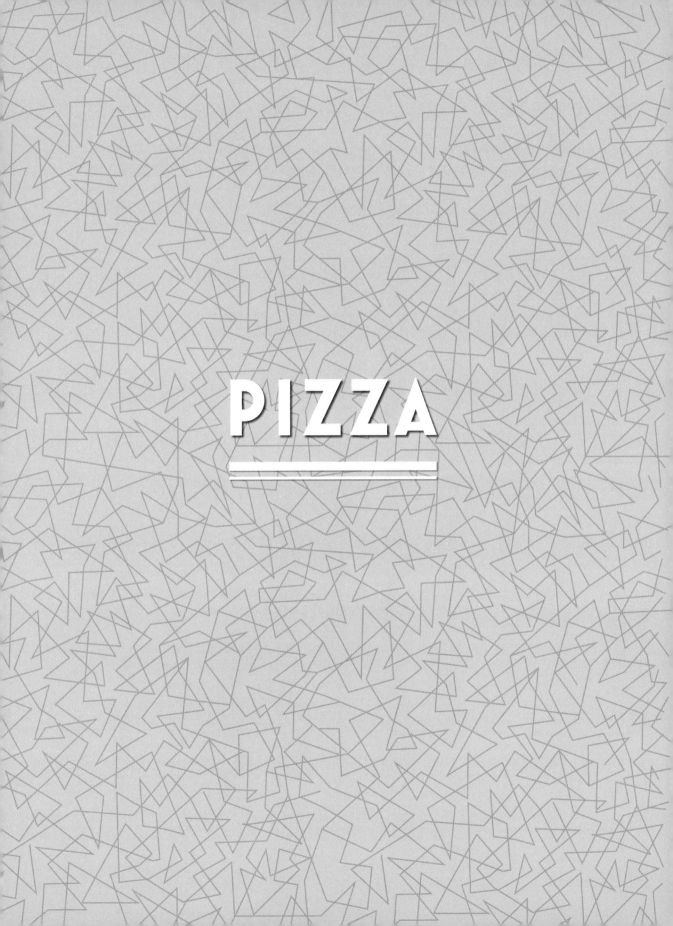

PIZZA

I WAS BROUGHT UP ON PIZZA and I can't actually remember it not being on our family menu at least three times a week. I know I'm biased as Naples is my home patch, but Neapolitan pizza is something really special. It originated there, so it's obviously going to be the best in the world, and every time I visit, it's one of the first things I eat. It is also incredibly easy to make and is actually great fun. My children love our regular pizza day. We all choose our toppings and put them in bowls, then we make our dough, and when it's ready we get cracking. They always say it's one of their favourite things to do, so if you are stuck for a lunch or dinner and your kids are bored, try it!

There are many famous pizzerias in Naples, most of them in the ancient historical centre. Most abide by the guidelines for true Neapolitan pizza established by the AVPN (Associazione Verace Pizza Napoletana), a regulatory body that has been set up to ensure quality control in making pizzas. (The association also selects pizzerias all around the world to produce and spread the *verace pizza Napoletana* philosophy.) The rules, which most of us follow, specify that the pizza must be baked in a wood-fired domed oven; that the base must be hand-kneaded and stretched, not rolled with a pin or prepared by any mechanical means; and that the pizza must not exceed 35cm in diameter or be more than 3mm thick at the centre. Some pizzerias go even further, however, using only San Marzano tomatoes grown on the slopes of Mount Vesuvius, and insist on adding the tomato topping and the drizzled olive oil in just a clockwise direction.

Pizza was originally a dish for poor people and was disdained by the better-off. It was sold in the street from open-air stands, and today many pizzerias in Italy still keep this tradition alive. It is now classified as a type of bread and tomato dish, often served with cheese, but until the early 20th century, pizza was sweet rather than savoury. Some traditional establishments, such as the famous Da Michele pizzeria in Via C. Sersale (founded in 1870), consider there to be only two true pizzas – the Marinara and the Margherita – and that is all they serve. Inevitably, there is no way I could not include these two 'pure' pizzas in this book, although there have been many amazing variations since they first came into being. It's the Margherita in particular that holds a special place in every Italian's heart, probably because of its national associations. The story goes that a Neapolitan restaurateur created it in the early 19th century to celebrate the visit of Queen Margherita, the first Italian monarch since Napoleon conquered Italy. The pizza included three ingredients that represented the colours of the new Italian flag: red (tomato sauce), white (mozzarella cheese), and green (fresh basil leaves).

As strong as traditions are, however, new styles of pizza are hitting Naples. The Pizza Metro chain, with its metre-long creations, has been around for a while now, but one restaurant I recently visited fries the pizzas rather than baking them. They look like giant flying saucers as they go into the hot oil. As a fan of tradition, I was sceptical of this development, but I must admit they tasted delicious – crispy outside and soft on the inside.

Traditional or modern, the main ingredient for a pizza topping is still tomatoes. You can use them in whichever form you like, but the traditional and most popular is chopped. (I like to use a mixture of chopped tomatoes and passata.) Tomatoes were originally eaten almost exclusively by the poor, but all that changed with the invention of the pizza Margherita. Today the tomato can justifiably claim to be the most popular fruit/vegetable in Italy.

Despite their poor reputation in the early days, tomatoes are now highly valued as a rich source of nutrients. In recent years, their abundant lycopene content has made many headlines for its disease-fighting abilities. Regardless of that, tomatoes look good and taste great, so they are already a big hit as far as most people are concerned.

While researching pizza information for this chapter, I learnt how basic ingredients (flour, tomatoes and herbs) can be combined to create something truly fantastic and prove what I have always preached – that simple, good-quality ingredients will always give you an amazing dish.

Please try to make my pizzas – you will find it so satisfying, and the taste will beat anything you buy off the shelf.

MARINARA

MARINARA

Pizza Topped with Anchovies, Garlic and Oregano

The marinara is one of the oldest pizza recipes in existence, being the traditional food prepared by *la marinara*, the fisherman's wife. I call it a Marmite recipe because you are either going to love it or hate it. Why? The anchovies. Personally, I can't get enough of this pizza, and think the flavours are incredible – every bite is amazing. To me, garlic and olives are already winners, and adding capers and anchovies just makes it even more heavenly. Take care to drain them thoroughly, though, or your pizza runs the risk of being soggy.

~~~~~~~~~~~~~~~~~~~~~~~~

Makes 2 pizzas

200G STRONG WHITE FLOUR, PLUS EXTRA FOR DUSTING

7G FAST-ACTION DRIED YEAST

PINCH OF SALT

140ML WARM WATER

3–4 TABLESPOONS EXTRA VIRGIN OLIVE OIL FOR GREASING/ BRUSHING

For the topping

150G PASSATA (SIEVED TOMATOES)

150G TINNED CHOPPED TOMATOES

4 TABLESPOONS EXTRA VIRGIN OLIVE OIL

1 TEASPOON DRIED OREGANO

50G SALTED CAPERS, RINSED AND ROUGHLY CHOPPED

10 ANCHOVY FILLETS IN OIL, DRAINED

20 KALAMATA PITTED BLACK OLIVES, HALVED

3 GARLIC CLOVES, PEELED AND SLICED

SALT AND BLACK PEPPER TO TASTE

First make the topping. Pour the passata and chopped tomatoes into a medium-sized bowl with 2 tablespoons of the oil. Mix in the oregano and capers and season with salt and pepper. Set aside at room temperature.

Prepare 2 baking trays by pouring a tablespoon of oil on each and spreading it out with your fingers or a pastry brush. Brush the inside of a large bowl with 1 tablespoon of oil and set aside.

To prepare the dough, place the flour, yeast and salt in a large clean bowl, make a well in the centre and pour in the water plus 2 tablespoons of the oil. Mix with a wooden spoon to create a wet dough.

Turn the dough onto a clean, well-floured surface and work it with your hands for about 5 minutes until smooth and elastic. Shape into a large ball and place in the oiled bowl. Brush the top of the dough with a little oil and cover with cling film. Leave to rest at room temperature for 20 minutes.

Preheat the oven to 200°C/gas mark 6.

Turn the rested dough onto a well-floured surface and divide it in half. Roll each piece into a ball, then push outwards from the centre to create 2 circles about 25cm in diameter. Place them on the oiled baking trays.

Spread the tomato mixture evenly over the pizza bases. (The best way to do this is to pour it in the middle and spread it outwards using the back of a tablespoon.)

Dot the anchovies and olives over the pizza bases and drizzle 1 tablespoon of the remaining oil over each one. Bake in the middle of the oven for 16 minutes, scattering the garlic over the top 2 minutes before the end.

Serve hot, sprinkled with a few basil leaves, and enjoy with a glass of Italian white wine

CAPRICCIOSA

PIZZA TOPPED WITH MOZZARELLA, OLIVES, MUSHROOMS AND HAM

Capricciosa means 'the naughty one', and this pizza is so called because it was created to please everybody. Perfect for a starter, great in a packed lunch, delicious if you are watching a movie... I've even been known to eat it cold for breakfast after a heavy night. Yum yum!

~~~~~~~~~~~~~~~~~~~~

Makes 2 pizzas

200G STRONG WHITE FLOUR, PLUS EXTRA FOR DUSTING

7G FAST-ACTION DRIED YEAST

PINCH OF SALT

140ML WARM WATER

3-4 TABLESPOONS EXTRA VIRGIN OLIVE OIL FOR GREASING/BRUSHING

For the topping

7 TABLESPOONS EXTRA VIRGIN OLIVE OIL

150G CHESTNUT MUSHROOMS, SLICED

300G PASSATA (SIEVED TOMATOES)

2 MOZZARELLA BALLS, DRAINED AND CUT INTO 1CM CUBES

20 PITTED GREEN OLIVES, HALVED

8 FRESH BASIL LEAVES

6 SLICES OF COOKED HAM, CUT INTO STRIPS

SALT AND BLACK PEPPER TO TASTE

First make the topping. Heat 3 tablespoons of the oil in a frying pan over a medium heat and fry the mushrooms for 5 minutes, stirring occasionally, until tender. Set aside to cool.

Prepare 2 baking trays by pouring a tablespoon of oil on each and spreading it out with your fingers or a pastry brush.Brush the inside of a large bowl with 1 tablespoon of oil and set aside.

To prepare the dough, place the flour, yeast and salt in a large clean bowl, make a well in the centre and pour in the water plus 2 tablespoons of the oil. Mix with a wooden spoon to create a wet dough.

Turn the dough onto a clean, well-floured surface and work it with your hands for about 5 minutes until smooth and elastic. Shape into a large ball

and place in the oiled bowl. Brush the top of the dough with a little oil and cover with cling film. Leave to rest at room temperature for 20 minutes.

Preheat the oven to 200°C/gas mark 6.

Turn the rested dough onto a well-floured surface and divide it in half. Roll each piece into a ball, then push outwards from the centre to create 2 circles about 25cm in diameter. Place them on the oiled baking trays.

Spread the passata evenly over the pizza bases. (The best way to do this is to pour it in the middle and spread it outwards using the back of a tablespoon.) Season with salt and pepper.

Divide the mozzarella, mushrooms and olives between the bases, then drizzle 2 tablespoons of oil over each of them.

Bake in the middle of the oven for 16 minutes, scattering the ham and basil over the top 2 minutes before the end of the cooking time. (For a vegetarian version, simply omit the ham.)

Serve hot and enjoy!

FIORENTINA

PIZZA TOPPED WITH MOZZARELLA, SPINACH, EGG AND PARMESAN

The Fiorentina is a firm favourite in the D'Acampo house, and always creates arguments over who gets the last piece. (My eldest son, Luciano, normally wins.) It's the healthiest pizza you can find, and this true classic from Florence is a great way of getting the whole family eating their greens.

~~~~~~~~~~~~~~~~~~~~~~~~~

Makes 2 pizzas

5 TABLESPOONS EXTRA VIRGIN OLIVE OIL, PLUS EXTRA FOR BRUSHING
200G STRONG WHITE FLOUR, PLUS EXTRA FOR DUSTING
7G FAST-ACTION DRIED YEAST
PINCH OF SALT
140ML WARM WATER

For the topping

300G FROZEN SPINACH, DEFROSTED
2 MOZZARELLA BALLS, DRAINED AND CUT INTO LITTLE CUBES
2 EGGS (THESE MUST BE REALLY FRESH)
60G FRESHLY GRATED PARMESAN CHEESE

Prepare 2 baking trays by pouring a tablespoon of oil on each and spreading it out with your fingers or a pastry brush. Brush the inside of a large bowl with 1 tablespoon of oil and set aside.

To prepare the dough, place the flour, yeast and salt in a large clean bowl, make a well in the centre and pour in the water plus 2 tablespoons of the oil. Mix with a wooden spoon to create a wet dough.

Turn the dough onto a clean, well-floured surface and work it with your hands for about 5 minutes until smooth and elastic. Shape into a large ball and place in the oiled bowl. Brush the top of the dough with a little oil and cover with cling film. Leave to rest at room temperature for 20 minutes.

Preheat the oven to 200ºC/gas mark 6.

Squeeze the spinach for the topping between your hands to remove any excess water. Set aside.

FIORENTINA

Turn the rested dough onto a well-floured surface and divide it in half. Roll each piece into a ball, then push outwards from the centre to create 2 circles about 25cm in diameter. Place them on the oiled baking trays.

Brush the top of each pizza base with 2 tablespoons of oil, then scatter with the mozzarella and spinach, leaving an empty 5cm circle in the centre. Bake in the middle of the oven for 8 minutes.

Remove the trays from the oven and crack an egg into the centre of each pizza. Continue baking for a further 8 minutes, scattering the Parmesan over the top 2 minutes before the end of the cooking time.

Serve and enjoy hot.

MARGHERITA

Pizza Topped with Mozzarella, Tomatoes and Fresh Basil

I know I've said this before but I really don't ever remember life without pizza. This wonderfully simple but full-flavoured pizza was originally created for the Queen Margherita of Italy, hence its name. A top tip is never to use dry herbs – fresh basil is a must – and make sure you don't use buffalo mozzarella as it's way too milky and will make your pizza base very soggy.

~~~~~~~~~~~~~~~~~~~~~~~~~~~

Makes 2 pizzas

5 TABLESPOONS EXTRA VIRGIN OLIVE OIL, PLUS EXTRA FOR BRUSHING

200G STRONG PLAIN FLOUR, PLUS EXTRA FOR DUSTING

7G FAST-ACTION DRIED YEAST

PINCH OF SALT

140ML WARM WATER

For the topping

150G TINNED CHOPPED TOMATOES

150G PASSATA (SIEVED TOMATOES)

2 TABLESPOONS EXTRA VIRGIN OLIVE OIL

13 FRESH BASIL LEAVES

2 MOZZARELLA BALLS, DRAINED AND CUT INTO LITTLE CUBES

SALT AND BLACK PEPPER TO TASTE

First make the topping. Pour the tomatoes and passata into a bowl and add the oil. Tear in 5 of the basil leaves, season with salt and pepper and set aside at room temperature.

Prepare 2 baking trays by pouring a tablespoon of oil on each and spreading it out with your fingers or a pastry brush. Brush the inside of a large bowl with 1 tablespoon of oil and set aside.

To prepare the dough, place the flour, yeast and salt in a large clean bowl, make a well in the centre and pour in the water plus 2 tablespoons of the oil. Mix with a wooden spoon to create a wet dough.

Turn the dough onto a clean, well-floured surface and work it with your

hands for about 5 minutes until smooth and elastic. Shape into a large ball and place in the oiled bowl. Brush the top of the dough with a little oil and cover with cling film. Leave to rest at room temperature for 20 minutes.

Preheat the oven to 200°C/gas mark 6.

Turn the rested dough onto a well-floured surface and divide it in half. Roll each piece into a ball, then push outwards from the centre to create 2 circles about 25cm in diameter. Place them on the oiled baking trays.

Spread the tomato mixture evenly over the pizza bases. (The best way to do this is to pour it in the middle and spread it outwards using the back of a tablespoon.)

Scatter the mozzarella evenly over the bases and bake in the middle of the oven for 16 minutes, scattering the remaining basil leaves over the top 1 minute before the end of the cooking time.

Serve hot and enjoy with your favourite cold beer.

AMALFI COAST

BIANCA

White Pizza Topped with Mozzarella, Gorgonzola, Parmesan and Fontina Cheese

This is dedicated to all you cheese-lovers. I have chosen my particular favourites, but you can use goat's cheese and Provolone as substitutes if you prefer. Be careful, by the way, not to order a pizza bianca in Italy as you will end up with something quite different – a white cheesy pizza with chips on top!

~~~~~~~~~~~~~~~~~~~~~~~~~~~~~~~~

Makes 2 pizzas

5 TABLESPOONS EXTRA VIRGIN OLIVE OIL, PLUS EXTRA FOR BRUSHING

200G STRONG WHITE FLOUR, PLUS EXTRA FOR DUSTING

7G FAST-ACTION DRIED YEAST

PINCH OF SALT

140ML WARM WATER

For the topping

2 TABLESPOONS EXTRA VIRGIN OLIVE OIL

2 MOZZARELLA BALLS, DRAINED AND CUT INTO SMALL CUBES

10G GORGONZOLA PICCANTE CHEESE, COLD AND CUT INTO SMALL CUBES

100G FONTINA CHEESE, COLD AND CUT INTO SMALL CUBES

60G FRESHLY GRATED PARMESAN CHEESE

8 FRESH BASIL LEAVES

SALT AND BLACK PEPPER TO TASTE

Prepare 2 baking trays by pouring a tablespoon of oil on each and spreading it out with your fingers or a pastry brush. Brush the inside of a large bowl with 1 tablespoon of oil and set aside.

To prepare the dough, place the flour, yeast and salt in a large clean bowl, make a well in the centre and pour in the water plus 2 tablespoons of the oil. Mix with a wooden spoon to create a wet dough.

Turn the dough onto a clean, well-floured surface and work it with your hands for about 5 minutes until smooth and elastic. Shape into a large ball and place in the oiled bowl. Brush the top of the dough with a little oil and cover with cling film. Leave to rest at room temperature for 20 minutes.

Preheat the oven to 200°C/gas mark 6.

Turn the rested dough onto a well-floured surface and divide it in half. Roll each piece into a ball, then push outwards from the centre to create 2 circles about 25cm in diameter. Place them on the oiled baking trays.

Brush 1 tablespoon of oil over each of the pizza bases. Scatter the mozzarella, Gorgonzola and Fontina evenly over them and bake in the middle of the oven for 15 minutes, sprinkling the Parmesan and basil leaves over the top 1 minute before the end of the cooking time.

Serve hot and enjoy with your favourite glass of Italian white wine.

QUATTRO STAGIONI

FOUR SEASONS PIZZA TOPPED WITH HAM, ARTICHOKES, MUSHROOMS AND BLACK OLIVES

The classic version of the Four Seasons pizza always includes artichokes. They are among the oldest medicinal plants in the world and are great for keeping the digestive system, eyes and cholesterol levels in good order. They also have an amazing flavour. I really like the idea that I am simulaneously looking after your taste buds and your health!

~~~~~~~~~~~~~~~~~~

Makes 2 pizzas

4 TABLESPOONS EXTRA VIRGIN OLIVE OIL, PLUS EXTRA FOR BRUSHING

200G STRONG WHITE FLOUR, PLUS EXTRA FOR DUSTING

7G FAST-ACTION DRIED YEAST

PINCH OF SALT

140ML WARM WATER

For the topping

3 TABLESPOONS EXTRA VIRGIN OLIVE OIL

100G CHESTNUT MUSHROOMS, SLICED

300G PASSATA (SIEVED TOMATOES)

2 MOZZARELLA BALLS, DRAINED AND CUT INTO SMALL CUBES

100G KALAMATA PITTED OLIVES, HALVED

4 SLICES OF PARMA HAM

4 ARTICHOKE HEARTS IN OIL, DRAINED AND CUT INTO QUARTERS

SALT AND BLACK PEPPER TO TASTE

First make the topping. Heat the oil in a frying pan over a medium heat and fry the mushrooms for 5 minutes, stirring occasionally, until tender. Set aside.

Prepare 2 baking trays by pouring a tablespoon of oil on each and spreading it out with your fingers or a pastry brush. Brush the inside of a large bowl with 1 tablespoon of oil and set aside.

To prepare the dough, place the flour, yeast and salt in a large clean bowl, make a well in the centre and pour in the water plus 2 tablespoons of the oil. Mix with a wooden spoon to create a wet dough.

Turn the dough onto a clean, well-floured surface and work it with your

hands for about 5 minutes until smooth and elastic. Shape into a large ball and place in the oiled bowl. Brush the top of the dough with a little oil and cover with cling film. Leave to rest at room temperature for 20 minutes.

Preheat the oven to 200°C/gas mark 6.

Turn the rested dough onto a well-floured surface. Take 2 little pieces of it and roll them into strings 44cm long. Cut them in half and set aside.

Divide the remaining dough in half and roll the pieces into really thin rectangles. Using the rolling pin to support them, carefully place them on the oiled baking trays.

Spread the passata evenly over the pizza bases. (The best way to do this is to pour it into the middle and spread it outwards using the back of a tablespoon.) Season with a little salt and pepper.

Scatter the mozzarella evenly over the bases, then form a cross on top of each one with 2 of the dough strings. Press the ends of the strings onto the edge of the base to secure. You will now have 4 roughly triangular areas to top with different fillings. Fill one triangle with olives, one with Parma ham, one with artichokes and one with mushrooms. Repeat this process to make the second pizza.

Bake in the middle of the oven for 16 minutes until golden brown.

Serve hot with a glass of Italian red wine.

VEGETARIANA
Pizza Topped with Sautéed Vegetables

I must admit, I probably wouldn't choose a vegetarian dish over a meat or fish one but in this case, I would definitely be tempted. Adding roasted vegetables to a pizza works amazingly well, so even if you aren't vegetarian, try this recipe. Also try topping it with slices of artichokes preserved in oil – it's really flavoursome.

~~~~~~~~~~~~~~~~~~~~~~~~~

Makes 2 pizzas

5 TABLESPOONS EXTRA VIRGIN OLIVE OIL, PLUS EXTRA FOR BRUSHING

200G STRONG WHITE FLOUR, PLUS EXTRA FOR DUSTING

7G FAST-ACTION DRIED YEAST

PINCH OF SALT

140ML WARM WATER

For the topping

6 TABLESPOONS EXTRA VIRGIN OLIVE OIL

100G CHESTNUT MUSHROOMS, SLICED

1 RED PEPPER, TRIMMED, DESEEDED AND CUT INTO 5MM STRIPS

1 YELLOW PEPPER, TRIMMED, DESEEDED AND CUT INTO 5MM STRIPS

1 LARGE COURGETTE, TRIMMED AND SLICED INTO 5MM DISCS

300G PASSATA (SIEVED TOMATOES)

2 MOZZARELLA BALLS, DRAINED AND CUT INTO SMALL CUBES

SALT AND BLACK PEPPER TO TASTE

First make the topping. Heat the oil in a large frying pan over a medium heat and fry the mushrooms, peppers and courgette for 8 minutes, stirring occasionally, until tender. Season with salt and pepper and set aside.

Prepare 2 baking trays by pouring a tablespoon of oil on each and spreading it out with your fingers or a pastry brush. Brush the inside of a large bowl with 1 tablespoon of oil and set aside.

To prepare the dough, place the flour, yeast and salt in a large clean bowl, make a well in the centre and pour in the water plus 2 tablespoons of the oil. Mix with a wooden spoon to create a wet dough.

Turn the dough onto a clean, well-floured surface and work it with your hands for about 5 minutes until smooth and elastic. Shape into a large ball and place in the oiled bowl. Brush the top of the dough with a little oil and cover with cling film. Leave to rest at room temperature for 20 minutes.

Preheat the oven to 200°C/gas mark 6.

Turn the rested dough onto a well-floured surface and divide it in half. Roll each piece into a ball, then push outwards from the centre to create 2 circles about 25cm in diameter. Place them on the oiled baking trays.

Spread the passata evenly over the pizza bases. (The best way to do this is to pour it into the middle and spread it outwards using the back of a tablespoon.) Season with a little salt and pepper.

Scatter the mozzarella and prepared vegetables evenly over the bases. Bake in the middle of the oven for 16 minutes until golden and crispy.

Serve hot.

CALZONE

Folded Pizza Stuffed with Mozzarella, Basil, Peppers and Salami Napoli

My late father, Ciro, absolutely loved this recipe and always ordered it when we went to a pizzeria, so it has to be in my pizza section. The word *calzone* actually means 'pair of trousers', but where that comes from I don't know. The key to a good calzone is to seal the edges properly. Once you have tried this basic recipe, be creative – anything goes.

~~~~~~~~~~~~~~~~~~~~~~~~

Makes 2 calzone

5 TABLESPOONS EXTRA VIRGIN OLIVE OIL, PLUS EXTRA FOR BRUSHING
200G STRONG WHITE FLOUR, PLUS EXTRA FOR DUSTING
7G FAST-ACTION DRIED YEAST
PINCH OF SALT
140ML WARM WATER

For the stuffing

3 TABLESPOONS EXTRA VIRGIN OLIVE OIL
2 RED PEPPERS, TRIMMED, DESEEDED AND CUT INTO 5MM STRIPS
300G PASSATA (SIEVED TOMATOES)
2 MOZZARELLA BALLS, DRAINED AND CUT INTO LITTLE CUBES
10 FRESH BASIL LEAVES
12 SLICES OF SALAMI NAPOLI
SALT AND BLACK PEPPER TO TASTE

First make the stuffing. Heat the oil in a large frying pan over a medium heat and gently fry the peppers for 6 minutes, stirring occasionally, until softened. Season with a little salt and pepper, then set aside to cool.

Prepare 2 baking trays by pouring a tablespoon of oil on each and spreading it out with your fingers or a pastry brush. Brush the inside of a large bowl with 1 tablespoon of oil and set aside.

To prepare the dough, place the flour, yeast and salt in a large clean bowl, make a well in the centre and pour in the water plus 2 tablespoons of the oil. Mix with a wooden spoon to create a wet dough.

Turn the dough onto a clean well-floured surface and work it with your

hands for about 5 minutes until smooth and elastic. Shape into a large ball and place in the oiled bowl. Brush the top of the dough with a little oil and cover with cling film. Leave to rest at room temperature for 20 minutes.

Preheat the oven to 200°C/gas mark 6.

Turn the rested dough onto a well-floured surface and divide it in half. Roll each piece into a ball, then push outwards from the centre to create 2 circles about 22cm in diameter. Place them on the oiled baking trays.

Spread 200g of the passata over just half the surface of each pizza base using the back of a tablespoon. Arrange the mozzarella, basil, peppers and salami on top, then fold the empty half of each base over to enclose the filling. Pinch the edges to seal, and turn them inwards, making tucks at regular intervals, to create a rope-like effect.

Bake in the middle of the oven for 14 minutes, then brush the top of each calzone with 2 tablespoons of oil and cover with the remaining passata. Bake for a further 2 minutes.

Serve hot.

* * * * * * * * * * * * * * * *

I LOVE MEAT – ALL KINDS OF MEAT – and although there are some fantastic vegetarian recipes around, I would really miss it if it wasn't in my weekly menu. In Italy we cure a lot of our meat, especially pork, though other meats, such as beef, veal, goat, chamois, venison, lamb, wild boar and (rarely) horse meat, are also used in this way. Cured meats, or *salumi*, have been around for centuries, and were invented out of a need to preserve meat for months. All cured meats must undergo salting first, and are then either air-dried or smoked. Spiciness will vary depending on the region (southern Italian *salumi* are generally more heavily spiced with black pepper, red pepper and chilli flakes than northern Italian versions). We often use these cuts of meat as antipasti or in sandwiches (see page 14).

Italians have been making an amazing array of cured meats for thousands of years. The ancient Romans prized the spicy pork sausages crafted in the southern region of Basilicata, and, being fond of intensely tasty foods, they smoked or salted whole pig thighs to yield savoury *prosciutti* that were not unlike those still made in mountain villages across Italy today. Two thousand years later, pork remains Italy's favourite meat for curing.

Italian *salumi* fall into two categories: those obtained from a whole cut of meat, such as a boneless thigh or shoulder (as in prosciutto, pancetta and coppa, etc.), and those obtained from minced, ground or chopped meat that is stuffed into casings, known as *insaccati* (as in salami, sausages, etc.). The best place to discover this incredible range of cured meats is in any *salumeria*, Italy's take on the delicatessen. There is an amazing example in Rome called Volpetti, where there are cured meats galore. I went there to buy pancetta for a classic carbonara that I was to cook in front of the Colosseum, but quickly decided to do it differently and ended up buying both pancetta and guanciale (cured pig's cheeks). It was amazing and resulted in the best carbonara I have ever made – and it wasn't a bad backdrop for cooking either!

Italian *salumi* can be rather expensive, and you might be wondering whether products from other countries, which are often cheaper, can be used instead. I heartily recommend using Italian cured meats whenever possible because those produced elsewhere bear no comparison – the animals are raised in different environments, on different foods and then cured in different climates.

However, not all meats in Italy are cured. On a visit to Anna Dente, a classic Roman chef, I saw that the traditions and heritage of Roman cooking are kept alive and their principles still apply today. Cheaper cuts of meat, like oxtail, offal, belly pork and cheeks, are still as popular as they

ROME

TORRE DEL GRECO

* * * * * * * * * * * * * * * * *

were in Roman times, although they tend to require long, slow cooking, and fewer and fewer restaurants now cook with them.

If you want to see meat, especially pork, at its best, you must visit Ariccia, a small town just outside Rome that is dedicated to one dish – porchetta – whole gutted and boned pig that is stuffed with a fragrant mixture of fennel, rosemary, garlic and pork fat, and then spit-roasted until crispy on the outside and unbelievably tender inside. Small shops and restaurants, all cooking this dish, line the streets and the town's squares, and the smells are amazing.

In my opinion the only way to eat porchetta is in a crusty bread roll, and one little shop I visited served over 300 such rolls in the course of a weekend. It's a simple but high-quality product cooked to perfection, and the queue just rolls (excuse the pun!) out of the door. *Fantastico*!

I know that the British sit around the table on Sundays with a huge joint of roasted meat, with all the traditional trimmings, but for Italians, meat is just one of many courses. It's almost as if they just can't decide what to eat, so they cook a bit of everything, and I for one love it.

Today, more expensive cuts of meat that require less cooking, such as steaks, chicken breasts, lamb cutlets, sausages and veal, have become the main meats found in restaurants and Italian homes, but they are still treated with Italian simplicity. Whether coated in breadcrumbs, marinated and pan-fried, or simply roasted, the meat itself is very much the star of the dish.

As always, there are regional differences. In southern Italy, it's often the poorer cuts of meat that are used, and they are slow-cooked. It is important to say, however, that although the meat might be cheaper, it is not inferior. Southern Italians are masters of using what they have to achieve an optimal result. Northern Italy differs in a number of ways. Most traditional north Italian recipes call for unsalted butter rather than olive oil, and beef, veal and pork are the meats of choice, with lamb and other animals playing a lesser role. Cooking ranges from boiling and frying through slow-braising and stewing. In the case of the latter, northern cooks use much less tomato, preferring to use wine or broth as the liquid, and chopped herbs for flavour. Finally, central Italy does have braised meats and stews but in much of the region the centrepiece of a classic holiday meal will be a platter of mixed, grilled or roasted meats, with poultry, pork, and beef, especially in Tuscany, where the renowned Chianina cattle graze the fields. In Lazio, on the other hand, the platter will probably also have lamb, which may also be present in Umbria and the Marche.

I've chosen a few of my favourite meat dishes that I make regularly at home and hope that you enjoy them as much as we do.

COSTOLETTE DI AGNELLO CON ROSMARINO E MIELE

Lamb Cutlets with a Honey and Rosemary Sauce

Inspired by the authentic Roman cooking of Anna Dente, this dish reflects the Romans' love of meat and all things sweet.

~~~~~~~~~~~~~~~~~~~~~~~

Serves 6

12 LAMB CUTLETS, FRENCH-TRIMMED
1 TABLESPOON OLIVE OIL
SALT AND PEPPER TO TASTE

For the dressing
1 TEASPOON HONEY
JUICE OF · LEMON
3 TABLESPOONS EXTRA VIRGIN
   OLIVE OIL

1 TABLESPOON FRESHLY CHOPPED
   FLAT LEAF PARSLEY

For the salad
2 SMALL FENNEL BULBS
12 WAFER-THIN SLICES OF PANCETTA

For the sauce
3 TABLESPOONS HONEY
2 FRESH ROSEMARY SPRIGS

First make the dressing. Mix the honey and lemon juice together in a bowl, then gradually whisk in the olive oil and 1 teaspoon of water. Stir in the parsley and season to taste.

To make the salad, finely slice the fennel and place in a bowl. Tear the pancetta, add to the bowl and drizzle over the dressing. Set aside.

Heat a griddle pan on a high heat. Drizzle the cutlets with olive oil and season with salt and pepper. Griddle for 1–2 minutes on each side, depending on thickness. Leave to rest for a couple of minutes on a plate.

To make the sauce, warm the honey and rosemary in a small pan on a low heat for 2 minutes. Season with black pepper.

Place the salad in the centre of your plate, then place 2 cutlets on top. Drizzle over the honey sauce and serve.

COSTOLETTE DI AGNELLO CON ROSMARINO E MIELE

BISTECCA CON SALSA DI ERBE FRESCHE

BISTECCA CON SALSA DI ERBE FRESCHE

Steak with Herby Sauce

This is my supper of choice for a boys' night in. Nothing quite beats a good-quality steak served with a simple herby sauce, and, because boys will be boys, there is always a bowl of my Italian roast potatoes to go with it instead of chips!

~~~~~~~~~~~~~~~~~~~~~~~~~~~~~~~~

Serves 4

4 RUMP STEAKS, ABOUT 200G EACH
OLIVE OIL
SALT AND BLACK PEPPER TO TASTE

For the sauce
SMALL BUNCH OF FRESH PARSLEY
SMALL BUNCH OF FRESH BASIL
2 TABLESPOONS FRESH OREGANO
  LEAVES
1 TABLESPOON FRESH THYME LEAVES

1 TABLESPOON FRESH TARRAGON
  LEAVES
1 TEASPOON FRESH ROSEMARY
  LEAVES
1 GARLIC CLOVE, PEELED
2 TABLESPOONS SALTED CAPERS,
  RINSED
6 TABLESPOONS OLIVE OIL
JUICE OF ½ LEMON

Place a large frying pan over a very high heat. Put the steaks on a plate and drizzle with olive oil, using a brush or your fingers to spread it over both sides.

Fry the steaks (in batches if necessary) for 3–4 minutes on one side until golden brown, then turn and cook the other side for a couple of minutes or so, depending on how well done you want them. Transfer to a plate, leave to rest for 5 minutes, and season with salt and pepper.

To make the sauce, finely chop the herbs, garlic and capers, then add enough olive oil to loosen the mix to a spooning consistency. Season with lemon juice, salt and pepper.

Slice the steaks thickly and serve with a spoonful of the herb sauce poured over each one.

POLLO AL FORNO IN CROSTA DI SALE

WHOLE SALT-BAKED CHICKEN

Bear with me on this one... A salt crust is traditionally used when cooking fish, but I've used the technique here to create the most succulent chicken you will ever eat – and, no, it's not salty. The crust creates a mini oven, steaming the chicken inside. Although not cheap to make, it's divine and guarantees a big wow factor at the table.

~~~~~~~~~~~~~~~~~~~~~~~~~~~~~~~~~~~

Serves 6

1 LEMON, ZESTED THEN HALVED

BUNCH OF FRESH THYME, PLUS A FEW EXTRA THYME LEAVES

BUNCH OF FRESH PARSLEY

1 FREE RANGE CHICKEN, ABOUT 2KG

2KG ROCK SALT

1 TABLESPOON CRACKED BLACK PEPPER

2 EGG WHITES, LIGHTLY BEATEN

SALT AND BLACK PEPPER TO TASTE

Preheat the oven to 200°C/gas mark 6. Place the lemon halves and bunches of herbs in the cavity of the chicken: you want to create a blockage so that salt can't get inside.

Mix together the salt, lemon zest, thyme leaves, cracked pepper and egg whites. Add a small cup of water to form the texture of wet sand.

Line a baking tray with 2 large sheets of foil so that you create a surface twice the size of the tray. Place a layer of the salt mixture on the foil and place the chicken on top. Start packing the remaining salt all around the bird, bringing up the foil as you do so to keep the salt in place. When finished, scrunch the foil closed on top.

Roast for 2 hours, then remove from the oven, open a little hole in the top of the foil and leave to rest for 20 minutes.

Take the chicken to the table, peel back the foil and crack open the salt crust. Serve with salads as a show-stopping Sunday lunch.

POLLO AL FORNO IN CROSTA DI SALE

PETTI DI POLLO AL FORNO CON POMODORINI

TRAY-BAKED CHICKEN WITH TOMATOES AND OLIVES

Tray-bakes are the perfect way of cooking for a family.
They're quick and easy to prepare, and you can be inventive
with flavours.

~~~~~~~~~~~~~~~~~~~~~~~~~~

Serves 4

4 CHICKEN BREASTS, SKIN ON
250G CHERRY TOMATOES ON THE
  VINE, CUT INTO SMALL BUNCHES
6 GARLIC CLOVES, UNPEELED
4 FRESH ROSEMARY SPRIGS
2–3 TABLESPOONS OLIVE OIL

8 SLICES OF PANCETTA
100G PITTED BLACK OLIVES
SALT AND BLACK PEPPER TO TASTE
A FEW FRESH BASIL LEAVES TO
  GARNISH

Preheat the oven to 180°C/gas mark 4.

Place the chicken breasts in a roasting tray and add the bunches of cherry
tomatoes. Bash the garlic cloves in their skin and place in the tray along
with the rosemary. Drizzle everything with olive oil and season with salt
and pepper.

Pop everything into the oven for 10 minutes, then drape the pancetta
slices over the chicken and scatter in the olives. Bake for another
15 minutes, then set aside to rest for 5 minutes.

Put each chicken breast on a plate with some tomatoes, olives, garlic
and juices. Sprinkle with the basil leaves and serve.

PETTI DI POLLO AL FORNO CON POMODORINI

VITELLO BRASATO CON GREMOLATA

VITELLO BRASATO CON GREMOLATA
Braised Veal Shanks with Parsley and Garlic Sauce

Veal is a popular meat in Italy, and the increasing availability of rose veal in the UK has seen it become more popular over here. It is a super-sweet meat, well worth trying.

~~~~~~~~~~~~~~~~~~~~~~~~~~~~~~~~~~~

Serves 4

4 TABLESPOONS OLIVE OIL

4 VEAL SHANK STEAKS, ABOUT 250G
EACH

1 ONION, PEELED AND FINELY
CHOPPED

2 CARROTS, PEELED AND FINELY
CHOPPED

2 CELERY STICKS, FINELY CHOPPED

A FEW FRESH THYME AND
ROSEMARY SPRIGS

1 BAY LEAF

2 TABLESPOONS TOMATO PURÉE

2 TABLESPOONS PLAIN FLOUR

150ML RED WINE

300ML BEEF, VEAL OR CHICKEN
STOCK

SALT AND BLACK PEPPER TO TASTE

For the gremolata

5 TABLESPOONS FINELY CHOPPED
FLAT-LEAF PARSLEY

ZEST OF 1 UNWAXED LEMON

1 GARLIC CLOVE, PEELED AND FINELY
CHOPPED

Heat the oil in a large saucepan over a medium heat and fry the veal shanks for 5–10 minutes until brown on all sides (you might need to do this in batches). Remove the shanks from the pan and set aside.

Add the onion, carrots and celery and fry for 5 minutes until starting to colour. Add the herbs and tomato purée and cook for 1 minute before stirring in the flour. Cook for a further 2 minutes, then pour in the wine and stock. Mix well, then return the shanks to the pan. Cover and simmer gently for 3–4 hours (or pop it in the oven for 3 hours at 160°C/gas mark 3) until the meat is really tender. When ready, if the sauce is too thin, remove the shanks from the pan and simmer the liquid until thickened.

To make the gremolata, combine all the ingredients for it in a bowl.

Serve the shanks with some of the sauce and a sprinkling of zesty gremolata.

CARPACCIO DI MANZO CON SALSA GREMOLATA

THINLY SLICED BEEF WITH PARSLEY OIL DRESSING

Carpaccio of beef is one of those dishes that every Italian serves on a Sunday. Although fillet beef is expensive, it is cut into thin slices so it goes along way, making you look more generous than you really are! This recipe is ideal to have as part of buffet-style lunch or as a starter.

Serves 6-8 as a starter

500G PIECE OF FILLET BEEF
2 TABLESPOONS OLIVE OIL
SALT AND BLACK PEPPER TO TASTE
**LARGE HANDFUL OF ROCKET
   LEAVES TO SERVE**

For the herb dressing
LARGE BUNCH OF PARSLEY
2 GARLIC CLOVES, PEELED
1 TBSP SALTED CAPERS, RINSED
JUICE OF ½ LEMON
**4 TABLESPOONS EXTRA VIRGIN
   OLIVE OIL**

Heat a frying pan on a very high heat. Season the beef on a plate with salt and pepper, then drizzle with the olive oil and rub it all over to coat it fully. Place in the hot pan and cook for 2 minutes on each side until golden brown all over, including the ends.

Set aside to rest for 10 minutes. The beef can then be served straight away, or refrigerated overnight.

To make the dressing, finely chop the parsley, garlic and capers (by hand or in a food processor). Transfer to a bowl, add the lemon juice and olive oil and season well with black pepper and a little salt. The mixture should have the texture of a wet pesto.

Cut the beef into thin slices, then place them flat on a large platter.

Dress the rocket leaves with a little extra virgin olive oil and place in a pile in the centre of the beef. Drizzle the dressing over the top, then serve.

STUFATO DI MANZO

Italian Beef Stew with Yellow Peppers and Olives

You don't tend to think of hot places such as southern Italy having stews, but they are certainly popular during the winter. It is a true Italian sight - a big pot of stew, another of polenta, pasta or potatoes, plus crusty bread and olive oil. This is my aunt's recipe, and a family favourite on a cold winter's night.

~~~~~~~~~~~~~~~~~~~~~~

Serves 4

2 TABLESPOONS OLIVE OIL

400G STEWING BEEF, CUT INTO LARGE CUBES

1 ONION, PEELED AND THINLY SLICED

2 YELLOW PEPPERS, DESEEDED AND THINLY SLICED

PINCH OF DRIED CHILLI FLAKES

2 FRESH ROSEMARY SPRIGS

1 X 400G TIN CHOPPED TOMATOES

200ML CHICKEN STOCK

HANDFUL OF PITTED BLACK OLIVES

Heat the oil in a medium saucepan over a high heat and fry the cubes of beef in batches for a few minutes until brown. Transfer to a plate.

Fry the onions for 5 minutes until soft. Add the peppers, chilli and rosemary and fry for 2 minutes. Pour in the tomatoes and stock, stir well, then return the beef to the pan and add the olives. Cover and simmer gently for 2 hours (or place in the oven at 160°C/gas mark 3 for 2-3 hours) until the meat is tender. Add a little more stock if the stew starts to dry out.

When cooked, season with salt and pepper and serve with mashed potato or polenta.

MAIALE AL FORNO CON LATTE E ROSMARINO

ROASTED PORK LOIN IN MILK AND ROSEMARY

Cooking pork in milk is very traditional in Italy, and in true Italian style, no one minds what it looks like as long as it tastes good. It may not be the Sophia Loren of dishes, but the milk makes the meat beautifully tender.

~~~~~~~~~~~~~~~~~~~~~~

Serves 8

2 TABLESPOONS OLIVE OIL

2–3KG BONELESS PORK LOIN

100G UNSALTED BUTTER

2 ONIONS, PEELED AND QUARTERED, EACH QUARTER STUDDED WITH A CLOVE

2 LITRES FULL-FAT MILK

2 BAY LEAVES

1 TABLESPOON BLACK PEPPERCORNS

A FEW FRESH TARRAGON SPRIGS

JUICE OF 1 LEMON

1 TABLESPOON FRESHLY CHOPPED TARRAGON

6 SPRING ONIONS, TRIMMED AND FINELY SLICED

SALT AND BLACK PEPPER TO TASTE

Preheat the oven to 150°C/gas mark 2.

Heat the oil in a large flameproof casserole dish over a high heat. Season the meat, then brown it on all sides. Add the butter and onions and fry for 1 minute. Add the milk, bay leaves, peppercorns and rosemary, making sure the pork is completely covered in milk.

Place in the oven, uncovered, and roast for 1½–2 hours until the meat is tender. Transfer to a plate and keep warm.

Skim the excess fat off the milk, then return the pan to the heat and simmer the liquid until thickened. Season with lemon juice, salt and pepper, then stir in the tarragon and spring onions.

Carve the meat and serve with some of the cooking juices poured over.

ROME

COSCIA DI AGNELLO FARCITA CON FINOCCHIETTO

Slow-Roasted Leg of Lamb Stuffed with Rosemary, Fennel Seeds and Apricots

Food and family go together in Italy, and there is nothing better than when they come together for a roast. Lamb's strong flavour means it can handle punchy accompaniments. It can also be cooked in one of two ways: long and slow (my favourite), or quickly roasted for juicy, pink meat.

~~~~~~~~~~~~~~~~~~~~~~~~~~~~

Serves 6

1 LEG OF LAMB, ABOUT 2KG, DEBONED AND BUTTERFLIED
2 RED ONIONS, PEELED AND CUT INTO RINGS 1 CM THICK
2 TABLESPOONS OLIVE OIL
SALT AND BLACK PEPPER TO TASTE

3 ANCHOVY FILLETS IN OIL, DRAINED
1 TABLESPOON FINELY CHOPPED FRESH ROSEMARY
100G FRESH BREADCRUMBS
75G DRIED APRICOTS, FINELY CHOPPED

For the stuffing
1 TABLESPOON FENNEL SEEDS
2 TABLESPOONS OLIVE OIL
50G BUTTER
1 ONION, PEELED AND FINELY CHOPPED

For the gravy
1 TABLESPOON PLAIN FLOUR
100ML RED WINE
1 LITRE LAMB OR CHICKEN STOCK
1 TABLESPOON REDCURRANT JELLY

Preheat the oven to 200°C/gas mark 6.

First make the stuffing. Crush the fennel seeds in a mortar. Heat the oil and butter in a frying pan over a low heat and fry the onion and fennel seeds gently for 10 minutes until soft and aromatic.

Add the anchovies and rosemary and cook for 1 minute, then remove the pan from the heat and stir in the breadcrumbs and apricots. Mix well and season with salt and pepper.

Place the lamb on a board, flesh side up, opened out like a book. Spoon the stuffing along the centre (vertically) where the bone once was, then roll it up from the short end to enclose the stuffing. Tie it up with a few lengths of string.

Place the red onions in the bottom of a roasting tin and sit the rolled lamb on top. (Doing this prevents the underside of the lamb from overcooking.) Season the lamb and drizzle with olive oil. Place it in the oven and immediately lower the temperature to 160°C/gas mark 3. Roast for 3 hours until the meat is tender. Transfer to a plate and set aside to rest for 20 minutes, covered with foil.

To make the gravy, drain off most of the fat in the roasting tin, leaving just 1 tablespoon in the bottom. Add the flour and stir well over the heat for 2 minutes. Pour in the wine, then use a spatula to scrape up all the caramelised bits from the bottom of the pan.

Allow the wine to bubble for 2 minutes before adding the stock and redcurrant jelly. Stir well, then strain into a clean pan and simmer for 10 minutes. Season well.

Remove the string from the lamb, carve the meat into slices and serve with the gravy handed separately.

COTOLETTA DI POLLO CON SALSA PIZZAIOLA

CRISPY CHICKEN BREAST WITH PIZZA SAUCE

Having grown up around Naples, I am inevitably a pizza lover. As a child I could easily have eaten it every day and for every meal, but my mother refused to let me. She invented this dish using all the classic pizza ingredients – tomato sauce, bread and mozzarella – and turned it into this amazing dish.

Serves 4

2 EGGS

60G FRESHLY GRATED PARMESAN CHEESE

60G BREADCRUMBS, TOASTED

2 TABLESPOONS PLAIN FLOUR

4 SKINLESS, BONELESS CHICKEN BREASTS, ABOUT 100G EACH

50ML OLIVE OIL

2 MOZZARELLA BALLS, DRAINED AND SLICED

SALT AND BLACK PEPPER TO TASTE

DRIED OREGANO TO GARNISH

For the sauce

2 TABLESPOONS OLIVE OIL, PLUS EXTRA FOR DRIZZLING

2 GARLIC CLOVES, PEELED AND SLICED

2 X 400G TINS CHOPPED TOMATOES

2 TEASPOONS DRIED OREGANO

For the salad

4 HANDFULS OF MIXED SALAD LEAVES

JUICE OF ½ LEMON

2 TABLESPOONS EXTRA VIRGIN OLIVE OIL

First make the sauce. Heat 2 tablespoons of olive oil in a pan, add the garlic and fry for 1 minute. Add the chopped tomatoes and oregano, season with salt and pepper and simmer for 10 minutes until the mixture has reduced and thickened.

Meanwhile, beat the eggs in a bowl and season with salt and pepper.

Combine the Parmesan, breadcrumbs and flour on a plate or in a shallow dish.

Place the chicken breasts between two pieces of cling film, then use a rolling pin to bash them out until they are 5mm thick.

Dip each chicken breast in the egg, then coat with the Parmesan breadcrumbs.

Heat the oil in a large frying pan and cook the coated breasts for 3 minutes on each side until coloured and cooked through. Drain on kitchen paper.

Dress the salad leaves with the lemon juice, extra virgin olive oil, salt and pepper, then place in serving bowls.

Spoon the tomato sauce into the middle of 4 plates and top with the chicken breasts. Place slices of mozzarella on top of the chicken, scatter with a little more oregano, some black pepper and a drizzle of olive oil and serve with the side salad.

COTOLETTA DI POLLO CON SALSA PIZZAIOLA

PANCETTA DI MAIALE AL FORNO
SLOW-ROASTED PORK BELLY WITH RADICCHIO

Pork belly is a great cut of meat if you are feeding a crowd of people as it's relatively cheap to buy. It is naturally very fatty, so long, slow cooking is the way to go as it renders out most of the fat, leaving tender, succulent meat. Radicchio is a classic accompaniment to pork in Italy. Its bitter flavour cuts through the fat, and it's helped along here by the balsamic vinegar.

~~~~~~~~~~~~~~~~~~~~~~~~~~~~~~~~~~

Serves 6

2 ONIONS, PEELED AND QUARTERED

1.5KG FREE RANGE PORK BELLY, BONES REMOVED, FAT SCORED

1 TEASPOON FENNEL SEEDS, LIGHTLY CRUSHED

1 TABLESPOON SEA SALT

For the radicchio

2 RADICCHIO HEADS

2 TABLESPOONS OLIVE OIL

3 TABLESPOONS BALSAMIC VINEGAR

A FEW FRESH THYME SPRIGS. LEAVES ONLY

3 TABLESPOONS BALSAMIC VINEGAR

25G HAZELNUTS, HALVED

Preheat the oven to 220°C/gas mark 7. Place the onions in a roasting tin. Dry the skin of the pork with kitchen paper. Sprinkle with the fennel seeds and sea salt and rub well into the cuts. Place the pork on top of the onions and roast for 40 minutes. Lower the temperature to 160°C/gas mark 3 and cook for a further 3 hours.

Set the pork aside to rest in a warm place. Increase the oven temperature to 180°C/gas mark 4.

Cut each head of radicchio into 6 wedges and rinse under the tap. Shake dry, then place in a bowl. Sprinkle with the olive oil, vinegar and thyme, season with salt and pepper and toss together. Tip into a roasting tin and cook in the oven for 15-20 minutes until tender, then stir in the hazelnuts.

Cut the pork into 6 pieces. Serve with the radicchio and new potatoes.

PANCETTA DI MAIALE AL FORNO

SALSICCE E LENTICCHIE

SALSICCE E LENTICCHIE

ITALIAN SAUSAGES WITH BRAISED LENTILS

Here's a great alternative to the traditional British bangers and mash. Italian sausages tend to be highly flavoured with herbs and spices, such as fennel, which adds a perfect boost of flavour to this recipe.

~~~~~~

Serves 4

2 TABLESPOONS OLIVE OIL

8 ITALIAN PORK SAUSAGES

25G BUTTER

1 ONION, PEELED AND FINELY CHOPPED

1 CARROT, PEELED AND FINELY CHOPPED

1 CELERY STICK, FINELY CHOPPED

1 RED CHILLI, DESEEDED AND FINELY CHOPPED

200G DICED PANCETTA

200G ITALIAN GREEN LENTILS

SMALL GLASS OF WHITE WINE

300ML CHICKEN OR VEGETABLE STOCK

2 TABLESPOONS FRESHLY CHOPPED PARSLEY

SALT AND BLACK PEPPER TO TASTE

Heat the oil in a lidded frying pan. When hot, fry the sausages for about 10 minutes until browned. Set them aside on a plate.

Add the butter, onion, carrot, celery and chilli to the empty pan and fry on a medium to low heat for 10 minutes until starting to caramelise. Add the pancetta and fry for 5 minutes until crispy.

Rinse the lentils under cold water, then add them to the pan. Stir well, then pour in the wine. Allow to simmer and reduce to 2 tablespoons.

Pour in the stock, return the sausages to the pan, then cover and bring to a simmer. Cook gently for 40 minutes, adding more stock if needs be, until tender. Stir in the parsley and season with salt and pepper.

MEAT-FREE

* * * * * * * * * * * * * * * *

ALTHOUGH I DO LOVE MEAT AND FISH, it would be very easy to be a vegetarian in Italy. The choice of recipes available is vast, and the quality of the vegetables, pulses, beans and cheeses is so good that you would always be truly satisfied. In the old days, meat was a luxury item that not everyone could afford, especially in the more impoverished rural areas of the country, and this is still reflected in many of the classic recipes and regional specialities. Italy's menus offer a range of exciting side dishes, complete meals based on vegetables and various seasonal produce employed in numerous traditional preparations. Just think of the huge possibilities offered by the three magic Ps: pasta, pizza, polenta! And that isn't even taking into consideration the amazing rice options and wonderful variety of cereals and grains, pulses, legumes, vegetable sauces, hearty soups, delicious dairy products, and the natural fresh produce readily available in any market.

There was a time when, if you were a vegetarian or vegan visiting Italy and you tried to explain to an Italian that you excluded meat as a lifestyle choice, the concept would have been alien to him. Although this might still be true in small rural areas, the picture has drastically changed, and there has been a sharp increase in vegetarianism due to both ethical/religious reasons and health concerns. On average, vegetarians weigh 10 per cent less than their meat-eating peers, so the trend towards a meat-free lifestyle is growing fast in Italy.

It's just as well, then, that Italy produces such wonderful fruit and vegetables. The warm weather, combined with the importance attached to eating locally and seasonally, allows people to eat the best food on offer. If you want to cook with red peppers but they're not in season, you won't see them on any market stall. In the bigger cities they do import things, but in local markets you buy what's available, and this means you get fruit and veg picked at their ripest and on the stalls just hours later.

When I visited the market of Campo Dei Fiori in the centre of Rome you could smell the sweetness of the tomatoes and the perfume of fennel in the air. When ingredients are this good, their flavour hits before you even take your first bite. It's a good reason for keeping recipes simple, and it's easy to see why becoming a vegetarian is an excellent option.

The heat in the south of Italy means that cream is very rarely used there, and dishes are kept light and fresh. The punchy flavours of chilli, lemon and fresh herbs are used to keep vegetarian dishes interesting and healthy. Vegetarians are not limited to stuffed peppers and mushroom risotto – the possibilities are endless. Even for die-hard carnivores, one meat-free day a week is never a bad thing. Just try my posh 'beans on toast' (see page 40) for an amazing weekday, meat-free meal. They're a world away from the ones you get out of a tin!

I've included some of my vegetarian favourites in this book, but meat-eaters love them too. They include:

BRUSCHETTA: A traditional antipasto, this is toasted bread rubbed with oil and garlic and served with a variety of toppings. The most popular is tomato, but there is also a huge variety of vegetarian toppings, from pulses and cheeses to puréed vegetables. Although all accounts of bruschette's origins trace it back to Italy, the exact region and year of its birth is not known, but ancient Romans reportedly used to test the quality of freshly pressed olive oil by smearing it on a piece of fire-toasted bread for tasting, a custom that is now common in all major olive-oil producing regions of Italy, specifically Lazio, Tuscany and Umbria.

PIZZA: If you're vegetarian, you have lots of pizza options but for me, the simplest of them all, the classic Margherita (see page 114), is perfection. In general, though, if meat's not listed as a topping, it won't be on the pizza, so you can always be secure in your decisions. Do please make sure you understand what all the toppings are, though. Peperoni, for example, is peppers, not sausage (that's 'pepperoni') .

PASTA ALL'ARRABBIATA: As a vegetarian option, this is my favourite pasta dish of all time and we have it in our house at least once a week. As explained on page 70, *arrabbiata* means 'angry' and may refer to the heat of the chilli peppers in the recipe, but some have said the name alludes to the bright red colour of the sauce – the colour of an angry woman's face. This traditional Roman recipe is an affordable and healthy dish that oozes flavour and, when made properly, is heaven on a plate with very few calories attached.

RISOTTO & GNOCCHI: Risotto is a rice-based dish that's especially popular in Milan, Venice and the north. There are many variations to choose from and most of them are vegetarian. (My personal favourites are mushroom or asparagus.) Traditional gnocchi are made with potato, but other ingredients can also be used, so make sure you ask what they contain. On the island of Sardinia, for example, you can find tiny saffron-flavoured potato gnocchi, while in the Alto Adige near Austria they are often made with breadcrumbs.

CONTORNI/GRILLED VEGETABLES: *Contorni* means 'sides', and will always be on an Italian menu. This is usually where you'll find an abundance of raw or cooked vegetable dishes, from (depending on the season) grilled aubergine and roasted potatoes to boiled spinach. While these dishes are normally intended to accompany meat or fish, my vegetarian friends have often ordered several of the *contorni* options and enjoyed a wonderful meal, using fresh crusty bread to mop up the flavours.

Just from the few examples I've described, you can see that being vegetarian in the Italian cuisine is not only easy but also absolutely tempting, even to the biggest carnivore out there. If you are like me and have guests you don't know really well over for dinner, always choose one of the five selections outlined here. The meal will still be impressive, extremely filling and tasty, and you will be safe in the knowledge that you are catering for every kind of palate.

RISOTTO CON ZUCCA E SALVIA
BUTTERNUT SQUASH RISOTTO WITH SAGE BUTTER

Italians often eat a small plate of risotto after their antipasti, and this in turn is followed by a meat or fish main course, but risotto also makes an excellent meat-free dish in its own right. The perfect risotto should be creamy and 'run' on the plate rather than being a thick stodge piled up high. Don't stint on the constant stirring. It's this (and the butter) that gives the rice its creamy texture.

~~~~~~~~~~~~~~~~~~~~~~~~~

Serves 4

1 LARGE BUTTERNUT SQUASH
5 TABLESPOONS OLIVE OIL
1 LARGE ONION, PEELED AND FINELY
  CHOPPED
300G ARBORIO OR CARNAROLI RICE
1.2 LITRES WARM VEGETABLE STOCK,
  MADE WITH 2 STOCK CUBES
30G SALTED BUTTER

40G FRESHLY GRATED PARMESAN
  CHEESE
1 TABLESPOON FRESHLY CHOPPED
  SAGE LEAVES
SALT AND WHITE PEPPER TO TASTE

For the sage butter
40G UNSALTED BUTTER
12 SMALL FRESH SAGE LEAVES

Peel and deseed the butternut squash then cut into 1cm cubes. Place them on a roasting tray, drizzle with 2 tablespoons of the olive oil and season with salt and pepper. Place in the oven and roast for 40 minutes until the squash is tender.

Reserve half the cooked cubes. Place the other half in a blender and blitz to a smooth purée. (If you want to get rid of the darker caramelised bits from the purée, pass it through a fine sieve.) Set aside.

Heat the remaining oil in a large saucepan over a medium heat and fry the onion for about 5 minutes until softened.

Meanwhile, make the sage butter. Melt the unsalted butter in a small pan. When foaming, add the sage leaves and cook for 2 minutes. Set aside.

RISOTTO CON ZUCCA E SALVIA

Add the rice to the onions and stir constantly for 2 minutes so the grains toast in the oil. Stir in the butternut squash purée.

Now, over a medium heat so that the mixture is just bubbling, start adding the stock a ladleful at a time, stirring continuously until each ladleful is absorbed before adding the next one. It is ready when all the stock has been absorbed and the rice is cooked but still has a slight bite. (This will take about 18 minutes).

Remove the pan from the heat and stir in the salted butter very quickly for at least 15 seconds. This is very important as it will create a fantastic creamy texture.

Now stir in the reserved squash cubes, Parmesan and chopped sage leaves and season with salt and pepper. If the risotto needs loosening at this stage, add a little hot water or stock.

Serve the risotto in warm bowls and spoon over a little of the sage butter.

RISOTTO CON PISELLI, ASPARAGI E MENTA

PEA, ASPARAGUS AND MINT RISOTTO

Once you have cooked a basic risotto, you can invent your own combination of flavours. For my family, this particular combination is summer on a plate.

~~~~~~~~~~~~~~~~~~

Serves 4

BUNCH OF THIN ASPARAGUS SPEARS, CUT INTO 3CM PIECES
3 TABLESPOONS OLIVE OIL
1 LARGE ONION, PEELED AND FINELY CHOPPED
300G ARBORIO OR CARNAROLI RICE
1.2 LITRES WARM VEGETABLE STOCK, MADE WITH 2 STOCK CUBES

150G FROZEN PEAS, DEFROSTED
1 TABLESPOON FRESHLY CHOPPED MINT
30G SALTED BUTTER
100G FRESHLY GRATED PARMESAN CHEESE
SALT AND WHITE PEPPER TO TASTE
PARMESAN SHAVINGS TO SERVE

Blanch the asparagus in boiling salted water for 1 minute, then drain and refresh in cold water.

Heat the oil in a large saucepan over a medium heat and fry the onion for about 3 minutes, stirring occasionally. Add the rice and stir constantly for 2 minutes so the grains toast in the oil. Now, over a medium heat, so the mixture is just bubbling, start adding the stock a ladleful at a time, stirring continuously until each ladleful is absorbed before adding the next one.

When you have only a ladleful or so of stock left, stir in the asparagus, peas and mint. Add the remaining stock and stir until absorbed and the rice is cooked but still has a slight bite. (This will take about 18 minutes.)

Remove the pan from the heat and stir in the salted butter very quickly for at least 15 seconds. This is very important as it will create a fantastic creamy texture. Finally, stir in the grated Parmesan cheese and serve immediately with a few Parmesan shavings on top.

RISOTTO CON PISELLI, ASPARAGI E MENTA

STUFATO DI FAGIOLI CON POLPETTINE DI PANE

STUFATO DI FAGIOLI CON POLPETTINE DI PANE

ITALIAN BEAN STEW WITH BREAD DUMPLINGS

Stews don't have to be all about meat. This recipe is a perfect storecupboard winter supper.

~~~~~~~~~~~~~~~~~~~~~~~

Serves 4

2 TABLESPOONS OLIVE OIL

½ ONION, CHOPPED

2 PINCHES DRIED RED CHILLI FLAKES

1 TEASPOON FRESHLY CHOPPED ROSEMARY LEAVES

1 X 400G TIN CHOPPED TOMATOES

300ML VEGETABLE STOCK

200G TINNED BORLOTTI BEANS, DRAINED AND RINSED

200G TINNED CANNELLINI BEANS, DRAINED AND RINSED

2 TABLESPOONS FRESHLY CHOPPED PARSLEY

SALT AND BLACK PEPPER TO TASTE

For the dumplings

200G CIABATTA BREAD

200ML MILK

1 TABLESPOON FRESHLY CHOPPED PARSLEY

ZEST OF 1 UNWAXED LEMON

1 EGG, BEATEN

1 TABLESPOON PLAIN FLOUR

OLIVE OIL

Heat the oil in a large saucepan over a medium heat and fry the onion for 1-2 minutes. Add the chilli flakes and rosemary and cook for a further 2-3 minutes. Add the tomatoes and bring to a simmer. Cook gently for 5 minutes before adding the beans. Bring to the boil, then simmer gently for 10 minutes, adding a little water or stock if it becomes too thick.

To make the dumplings, cut the ciabatta into 1cm cubes and place in a bowl. Warm the milk, then pour it over the bread and leave it to soak for 10 minutes. Season with salt and pepper and stir in half the parsley, the lemon zest, egg and flour to make a sticky dough. If it is too wet, add a little more flour.

Shape the mixture into walnut-sized balls. Heat a little olive oil in a frying pan and fry the dumplings for 5 minutes until golden brown on all sides. Serve with the stew, sprinkling the remaining parsley over it.

AMALFI

GNOCCHI DI SPINACI E RICOTTA

GNOCCHI DI SPINACI E RICOTTA

RICOTTA AND SPINACH DUMPLINGS

Opinions differ about where the word 'gnocchi' derives from: some believe it comes from nocchio, meaning 'knot' (as in a plank of wood), or from nocca, meaning 'knuckle'. Both are plausible because the shapes are similar. The key thing to remember is that there are two types of gnocchi: potato and ricotta. Potato gnocchi are more time-consuming to make but you can now buy good-quality, ready-made ones in your local supermarket or deli. However, if you want to make your own and time is short, this quicker version is for you.

~~~~~~~~~~~~~~~~~~~~~~~~~~~~~~~~~~~~~~~

Serves 4

400G BABY SPINACH LEAVES, WASHED

250G RICOTTA CHEESE

2 LARGE EGGS, BEATEN

125G PLAIN FLOUR

125G FRESHLY GRATED PARMESAN CHEESE

A FEW FRESH BASIL LEAVES

SALT AND BLACK PEPPER TO TASTE

PARMESAN SHAVINGS TO SERVE

For the sauce

3 TABLESPOONS OLIVE OIL

2 GARLIC CLOVES, PEELED AND SLICED

600G CHERRY TOMATOES, HALVED

Place the spinach in a colander and blanch it by pouring over boiling water. When cool enough to handle, place it in a clean tea towel and squeeze out the excess water. Finely chop and set aside.

Place the ricotta in a bowl and stir to loosen. Add the eggs, spinach, a good pinch of salt, pepper, the flour and grated Parmesan. Mix well, then use lightly floured hands to roll the mixture into 20 walnut-sized balls. Transfer to a tray and refrigerate for at least 30 minutes.

Meanwhile, prepare the sauce. Heat the olive oil in a frying pan over a medium heat and fry the garlic for 1 minute before adding the halved tomatoes. Cook for 3–4 minutes until the tomatoes start to break down but still hold their shape. (You might need to add a splash of water to loosen the sauce.) Season with salt and pepper.

Bring a large shallow pan of salted water to the boil, then carefully drop the gnocchi into it. Lower the heat to a simmer and cook gently for 10 minutes until the gnocchi are cooked and float to the top.

Using a slotted spoon, transfer the gnocchi to the pan with the sauce. Tear a few of the basil leaves and stir them in.

Serve in warm bowls, finished with a few shavings of Parmesan, the remaining basil leaves, a drizzle of olive oil and a little fresh black pepper.

TORTA DI RICOTTA E PATATE CON MELANZANE

BAKED RICOTTA AND POTATO CAKE WITH ROASTED AUBERGINE

Vegetarians often get a raw deal when it comes to their choice of main courses at restaurants and dinner parties. Stuffed peppers or mushroom risottos are normally on the menu, but this is a delicious alternative using one of Italy's finest ingredients – ricotta cheese. Made from whey, a by-product from the making of other cheeses, ricotta is a soft, light curd cheese with a slightly grainy texture. Like most things Italian, it has regional variations, but its great virtue is its versatility, as it can be used in both savoury and sweet dishes.

~~~~~~~~~~~~~~~~~~~~~~~~~~~~~~

Serves 4

BUTTER FOR GREASING

500G FRESH WHOLE-MILK RICOTTA

2 LARGE EGGS

150G FRESHLY GRATED PARMESAN
  CHEESE

A FEW FINELY CHOPPED FRESH
  OREGANO LEAVES

1 RED CHILLI, DESEEDED AND FINELY
  CHOPPED

ZEST OF 1 UNWAXED LEMON

2 GARLIC CLOVES, PEELED AND
  GRATED

SALT AND BLACK PEPPER TO TASTE

SALAD AND TOASTED BREAD TO
  SERVE

For the aubergine

2 AUBERGINES

3 TABLESPOONS OLIVE OIL, PLUS
  EXTRA FOR DRIZZLING

ZEST AND JUICE OF ½ LEMON

½ TEASPOON CASTER SUGAR

A FEW FRESH BASIL LEAVES, TORN

25G PINE NUTS

Preheat the oven to 180°C/gas mark 4. Grease a loose-bottomed 10-15cm fluted tart tin or cake tin with butter and line with baking paper.

Place the ricotta in a bowl, then add the eggs, Parmesan, oregano, chilli, lemon zest and garlic. Mix well with a fork, then season with salt and pepper. Place the mixture in the prepared tin and spread it out evenly.

Bake for 25–30 minutes until golden and puffed up.

Meanwhile, thinly slice the aubergines, cut each slice in half lengthways and place in a non-stick baking tray. Drizzle with olive oil and season with salt and pepper. Place them in the oven and roast for 15 minutes until golden brown and soft.

Mix together the lemon juice, caster sugar and 3 tablespoons olive oil in a large bowl. Season with salt and pepper, then stir in the basil leaves.

Once the aubergines are cooked, add them to the basil dressing along with the pine nuts.

Transfer the torta to a plate and cut into wedges, like a cake. Serve with the roasted aubergines, a simple green salad and toasted ciabatta.

TORTA DI RICOTTA E PATATE CON MELANZANE

CRESPELLE AL FORNO

Baked Savoury Pancakes with Mushrooms, Spinach and Basil Pesto

This dish is not just for vegetarians. The meaty mushrooms and flavourful sauce ensure that even the manliest of carnivores will not miss meat.

~~~~~~~~~~~~~~~~~~~~~~~~~~~~~~

Serves 4

250G PLAIN FLOUR

3 EGGS, LIGHTLY BEATEN

500ML MILK

2 TABLESPOONS FRESHLY CHOPPED
  CHIVES

LIGHT OLIVE OIL FOR FRYING

SALT AND PEPPER TO TASTE

For the filling

2 TABLESPOONS OLIVE OIL

25G BUTTER

500G CHESTNUT MUSHROOMS,
  SLICED

2 GARLIC CLOVES, PEELED AND
  CRUSHED

300G SPINACH

100ML VEGETABLE STOCK

200G MASCARPONE CHEESE

1 TABLESPOON PLAIN FLOUR

1 TABLESPOON SOFT BUTTER

2 TABLESPOONS FRESHLY CHOPPED
  PARSLEY

4 TABLESPOONS PESTO

6–8 LARGE TOMATOES, SLICED

50G FRESHLY GRATED PARMESAN
  CHEESE

Place the flour in a large bowl. Add the eggs and start to incorporate them with a whisk while gradually pouring in the milk. When half the milk has been added, whisk vigorously to get rid of any lumps. When you have a smooth batter, whisk in the rest of the milk and the chives. Season with a little salt and pepper.

Heat a teaspoon of oil in a large frying pan over a medium-high heat. Use some kitchen paper to wipe out the excess, then pour in a ladleful of the batter. Tilt the pan to swirl the batter around so it covers the bottom. Cook for about 1 minute until set on top and golden brown on the base. Flip the pancake over and cook for 30 seconds on the other side. Remove from the pan and place on a sheet of baking paper.

Repeat this step with the remaining batter, making 8 pancakes in total and stacking them with baking paper in between to prevent them from sticking together. (If you like, the pancakes can be frozen at this stage for future; simply defrost when needed.)

To make the filling, heat the oil and butter in a large frying pan. Add the mushrooms and garlic and fry in 2 batches until golden brown. Transfer to a plate, then add the spinach to the pan. Cook until wilted. then return the mushrooms to the pan. Pour in the stock and stir in the mascarpone. Bring to a simmer.

Mash together the flour and soft butter, then stir into the mushroom filling to thicken the sauce. Simmer for a minute or so, then stir in the parsley and pesto. Season with salt and pepper.

Preheat the oven to 180°C/gas mark 4.

Take a pancake and place a few spoonfuls of filling in a line down the middle, fold in the ends then roll up so the pancake encases the filling. Place in a 23 x 33cm ovenproof dish and repeat with the remaining pancakes. Top with sliced tomatoes and sprinkle over the Parmesan.

Place the pancakes in the oven for 25 minutes until the cheese has melted, then serve.

FRITTATA DI ZUCCHINE CON SALSA DI POMODORI

FRITTATA DI ZUCCHINE CON SALSA DI POMODORI

COURGETTE FRITTATA WITH TOMATO AND GREEN OLIVE SALSA

Frittatas are one of my favourite lunchtime dishes. In Italy I cooked this recipe at Casolare da Tobia, a restaurant on the volcano just outside the city of Naples. The fertile soil in its garden yields the most delicious produce for the chefs.

~~~~~~~~~~~~~~~~~~~~~

Serves 4

2 TABLESPOONS OLIVE OIL
1 RED ONION, PEELED AND SLICED
3 COURGETTES (PREFERABLY WITH FLOWERS), SLICED
1 YELLOW PEPPER, AND SLICED
1 RED PEPPER, SLICED
6 EGGS, BEATEN
50G PARMESAN CHEESE
SALT AND PEPPER TO TASTE

For the salsa
4 RIPE TOMATOES, DICED
50G PITTED GREEN OLIVES, CUT IN HALF
2 TABLESPOONS OLIVE OIL
JUICE OF ½ LEMON
PINCH OF DRIED CHILLI FLAKES
SMALL BUNCH OF BASIL LEAVES, TORN

Heat the oil in a frying pan over a medium heat and add the onion and peppers. Cook for 2 minutes before adding the courgettes. Cook for 3–4 minutes until starting to brown. Season with salt and pepper.

Season the eggs with black pepper, then pour into the frying pan. Use a spatula to move them around until they start to set on the bottom and around the sides. Grate a little Parmesan over the frittata, then carefully slide it out onto a board or saucepan lid. Place the frying pan on top and flip it over so that you can cook the other side for 2 minutes. Grate a little more Parmesan over the top.

To make the salsa, put the tomatoes, olives, oil and lemon juice in a bowl, season with salt and pepper, then add the chilli flakes. Set aside for 10 minutes, then add the basil. Slide the cooked frittata onto a plate and serve with the salsa on top.

FISH

I REALLY CAN'T REMEMBER my life, even as a young boy, without having fish at least once a week. As you know, I am from the south of Italy, where seafood is so fresh and abundant that many people have it daily. With 5,000 miles of coastline, the sea is never too far away, and it offers us a huge selection of fish, such as sea bass, mullet, sea bream, tuna, sardines, swordfish, clams, mussels, lobster, octopus and squid. As for the four regions of Italy that aren't near the sea, they enjoy freshwater fish from their own lakes and rivers. Almost everything that lives in the sea finds its way to an Italian table, from swordfish, which the fishermen still harpoon from the bow of their boats in the Straits of Messina, to *arselle*, little clams, that live in the sand just beyond the shore and are gathered with strainers.

I used to love going fishing with my father. We had a small speedboat and would go out for hours. He would tie a hook onto a piece of rope, attach just bread as bait and throw it over the side. We never came home empty-handed, and my mother would put our catch on a barbecue and serve it with fresh vegetables or salad. Sometimes we would use nets, which my family would be thrilled about as it meant we would come home with buckets full of fish. I know they appreciated it more, but the hook and bread way of fishing gave my father and me much more satisfaction. Those are the days I will never forget, and the days I now continue to enjoy with my boys Luciano and Rocco.

Fish has always played a big role in Italian cuisine. During the 19th century the Catholic Church specified that fish should be eaten on Fridays and days of penitence, such as during Lent, and all large cities had fishmongers to meet this demand. To this day, many restaurants and households have maintained the tradition of meatless Friday.

Methods of fishing have changed over the years, but the technique used obviously depends on what you are trying to catch. One ancient method I find particularly interesting is called *trabucco*, which is the name of an old fishing machine. It was a massive wooden construction consisting of a platform anchored to coastal rocks by large logs jutting out into the sea. From the platform two or more long arms stretched out above the water and supported a huge, narrow-meshed net called a *trabocchetto*. The fishing technique consisted of using the net to intercept the flows of fish moving along the coastal ravines. The typical *trabucco* was located where the sea was at least 6 metres deep, and generally orientated southeast or north in order to exploit the favourable marine current. Some of these machines have been rebuilt and are now tourist attractions. Whatever method is used, Italians are still forbidden from catching fish smaller than 7cm in length.

* * * * * * * * * * * * * * *

I know I have mentioned regional differences in Italian cuisine before, but it still amazes me when I find out certain facts. For example, in the south of Italy we have been enjoying tuna steaks for centuries, yet in the north, tuna was only ever eaten from tins until the 1990s. The one constant throughout Italy is that most people still buy their fresh fish from fish markets. I love those hustle and bustle places; they are full of energy, with many of the stall-holders selling you the fish they have spent the night catching so you can go home and enjoy it that same evening. If you actually stop and chat to them, their stories are amazing – many of them still fish in small wooden boats and insist it's the only way to do it.

It is well known that eating fresh fish is one of the healthiest ways to make sure you and your family are getting your daily supply of proteins and minerals, so serving fish is always a wise choice. Compared to meat, poultry and even vegetables, fish is relatively economical, especially when used as part of a pasta dish. Many fish dishes are delicious and visually gorgeous while still being very easy and quick to prepare. Seafood, including salt-water fish, molluscs and shellfish, provide fantastic colour, texture and taste.

Fisheries and their spin-off industries are essential in Italy because of their role in providing food security and employment. The country ranks among the world's leading developed economies, especially in terms of food quality, so genetically modified crop production is banned, and many Italians are resistant to genetically modified aquaculture, whether it be fish or any kind of sea produce. Over the last three decades, reduced fish stocks and increased fishing restrictions have lowered the profile of the Italian fishing industry. Nonetheless, and despite fishermen's often low incomes, it is still economically significant because it provides local jobs and seafood production. In fact, consumer demand for seafood in Italy is higher than ever.

Like any kind of food, fish also has it seasons. You will find that some, such as swordfish and tuna, can be available all year round, but lobster is definitely a spring/summer delicacy, while sea trout and anchovies are more readily available in the autumn/winter months. Of course, with ways of preserving food for longer, and worldwide trading now the norm, many of us can enjoy any type of fish all year round.

For this chapter I have chosen some fish recipes that I know you will love. Not only are the flavours amazing but they are also some of the easiest meals you will ever prepare.

SPIGOLA AL CARTOCCIO
BARBECUED WHOLE FISH IN FOIL

If you're planning a barbecue, why not try something slightly more interesting than good old sausages and burgers? Cooking a whole fish on the barbecue is really quick and makes a great centrepiece to any summer table.

~~~~~~~~~~~~~~~~~~~~~~~~~~~~~~~~~~

Serves 4

1 LARGE SEA BASS, ABOUT 1.2KG, GUTTED, CLEANED AND SCALED

1 LEMON, THINLY SLICED

100G SOFT UNSALTED BUTTER

1 GARLIC CLOVE, PEELED AND CRUSHED

2 TABLESPOONS FINELY CHOPPED FRESH PARSLEY

1 TABLESPOON FINELY CHOPPED FRESH DILL

SALT AND BLACK PEPPER TO TASTE

Let the flames on your barbecue die down so that the embers are glowing white. At that point take 2 large pieces of foil and lay them on top of each other on a work surface. (Doubling up the foil helps to prevent it from tearing while cooking.)

Use a sharp knife to make 5 incisions into the skin of the sea bass, taking care not to cut too deep, then place the fish on the foil. Insert the lemon slices inside the body cavity and season with a little salt and pepper.

Mix together the butter, garlic, parsley and dill. Season with salt and pepper, then dot the mixture over the fish. Bring the sides of the foil up around the fish and fold along the top to seal.

Place the fish on the barbecue rack and cook for 15-20 minutes, depending on the heat of the coals and the size of the fish. When you think it's ready, carefully open the parcel and look inside the body cavity – the flesh should be firm and white.

Serve the fish in the foil, carefully peeling back the skin and removing the succulent flesh from the bones. Serve with the warm butter sauce poured over it.

SPIGOLA AL CARTOCCIO

SPIEDINI DI GAMBERONI E PANE

MARINATED PRAWNS AND CIABATTA KEBABS WITH FENNEL SALAD

This is not your usual Friday night kebab. Juicy succulent prawns with crispy ciabatta go perfectly with my Italian take on coleslaw.

~~~~~~~~~~~~~~~~~~~~~~~~~~~~~~~~~~~~~

Serves 4

24 LARGE UNSHELLED PRAWNS, HEADS REMOVED
½ STALE CIABATTA LOAF, CUT INTO 2CM CUBES
ZEST OF 1 UNWAXED LEMON
PINCH OF DRIED CHILLI FLAKES
4 TABLESPOONS OLIVE OIL
SALT AND BLACK PEPPER TO TASTE

For the fennel salt
½ TEASPOON FENNEL SEEDS
1 TEASPOON SEA SALT

For the salad
¼ WHITE CABBAGE, FINELY SHREDDED
1 FENNEL BULB, FINELY SHREDDED
HANDFUL OF ROCKET LEAVES
3 TABLESPOONS MAYONNAISE
1 TEASPOON WHOLEGRAIN MUSTARD
JUICE OF 1 LEMON

Place the prawns, ciabatta, lemon zest, chilli flakes, olive oil, salt and pepper in a large bowl. Toss everything together and leave to marinate for 30 minutes. Meanwhile, soak 8 wooden skewers in water.

Thread the prawns onto the skewers, alternating them with the ciabatta. Place on a hot griddle pan or barbecue. Cook for 3 minutes on each side until the prawns are pink and the bread is golden brown and toasted.

To make the fennel salt toast the fennel seeds for about 1 minute in a dry pan until aromatic, then grind them in a mortar. Add the sea salt.

To make the salad, put the shredded leaves and rocket in a bowl. Mix together the mayonnaise, mustard and lemon juice, season, then stir through the leaves. Serve the kebabs with a sprinkling of fennel salt and the fennel salad.

TONNO GRIGLIATO CON SALSA DI POMODORI E CAPPERI

Griddled Tuna Steaks with Tomato and Caper Salsa

Fresh tuna steak is completely different from the tinned tuna we mix with mayonnaise for sandwiches. If you're not keen on the tinned stuff, try the fresh – you might just like it.

~~~~~~~~~~~~~~~~~~~~~~~~~~~~~~~~

Serves 4

4 TUNA STEAKS, ABOUT 200G EACH
OLIVE OIL
SALT AND BLACK PEPPER TO TASTE

For the tomato and caper salsa
200G CHERRY TOMATOES,
  QUARTERED
1 SHALLOT, PEELED AND FINELY
  SLICED

1 TABLESPOON SALTED CAPERS,
  RINSED
1 TABLESPOON OLIVE OIL
2 TABLESPOONS GOOD-QUALITY
  BALSAMIC VINEGAR
200G TINNED ITALIAN OR PUY
  LENTILS, DRAINED
A FEW FRESH BASIL AND ROCKET
  LEAVES

First make the salsa. Place the tomatoes, shallot and capers in a bowl. Add the oil and vinegar and stir in the lentils. Season and set aside while you cook the tuna.

Heat a large frying pan over a high heat. Place the tuna steaks on a plate and drizzle with olive oil. Season on both sides, then add to the pan, 2 at a time. Cook for 1 minute, then turn over and cook for 30–60 seconds, depending on how well done you want them. Transfer to a plate and keep warm while you cook the other two steaks.

Add the basil leaves and rocket to the salsa and serve alongside the tuna with a drizzle of olive oil.

TAGLIATA DI PESCE CON SALSA DI PEPERONI DOLCI

Brill Roasted with Sweet Pepper Sauce

Brill is a large, firm-textured flat fish that is not used as often as it should be. If you can't get hold of it, try a similar fish, such as turbot, although it is more expensive.

~~~~~~~~~~~~~~~~~~~~~~~~~~~

Serves 4

4 BRILL FILLETS, ABOUT 180G EACH, SKIN ON
70G FRESH BREADCRUMBS
2 TABLESPOONS FRESHLY CHOPPED PARSLEY
ZEST OF 1 UNWAXED LEMON
50G BUTTER, MELTED

SALT AND BLACK PEPPER TO TASTE
FRESH BASIL LEAVES TO GARNISH

For the sweet pepper sauce
1 X 290G JAR ROASTED PEPPERS IN OIL
1 GARLIC CLOVE, PEELED AND SLICED
100ML FISH OR VEGETABLE STOCK

Preheat the oven to 200°C/gas mark 6.

First make the sauce. Place 1 tablespoon of the oil from the jar of peppers in a small pan. Heat gently over a low heat and fry the garlic for 1 minute. Drain the peppers and add them to the pan. Pour in the stock and bring to a simmer. Cook gently for 5 minutes, then transfer everything to a blender and blitz until smooth. Season with salt and pepper. Return the sauce to the pan and set aside.

Place the fish in a roasting tray, skin side down. Combine the breadcrumbs, parsley, lemon zest, melted butter and seasoning. Spoon the mixture on top of the fish and press down lightly to cover.

Roast in the oven for 12-15 minutes until the topping is golden brown and the flesh is opaque in the centre when touched with a knife.

Reheat the sauce, spoon it onto plates and put the fish on top. Sprinkle with the basil leaves and serve.

SPIGOLA IN PADELLA CON COUS COUS ALLE ERBE

SPIGOLA IN PADELLA CON COUS COUS ALLE ERBE

Crispy Fillet of Sea Bass with Herby Couscous

Fish and couscous are really quick to prepare, so this recipe is fast food at its best. The dish can be ready in less than 15 minutes, and its bright colours will liven up any table.

~~~~~~~~~~~~~~~~~~~~~~~~~~~

Serves 4

1 TABLESPOON OLIVE OIL
4 LARGE SEA BASS FILLETS, CUT IN
   HALF ACROSS THE MIDDLE

For the salsa
200G CHERRY TOMATOES,
   QUARTERED
HANDFUL OF PITTED BLACK OLIVES,
   QUARTERED
2 TABLESPOONS OLIVE OIL
SQUEEZE OF LEMON JUICE
SALT AND BLACK PEPPER TO TASTE

For the couscous
250G COUSCOUS
300ML BOILING CHICKEN OR
   VEGETABLE STOCK
2 TABLESPOONS OLIVE OIL
1 TABLESPOON CHOPPED FRESH
   HERBS, SUCH AS DILL, PARSLEY,
   CHIVES, ETC.
LARGE HANDFUL OF ROCKET LEAVES

First make the salsa. Combine all the ingredients for it in a bowl and add seasoning.

Place the couscous in a bowl, pour in the stock, then cover with cling film and leave to stand for 5 minutes. Fluff up the grains with a fork. Add the oil, herbs and seasoning. Leave to cool slightly while you cook the fish.

Heat the olive oil in a frying pan over a high heat. Season the fish fillets, then place them skin side down in the pan. Cook for 3 minutes until crispy, then turn and cook the flesh side for 1 minute.

Stir the rocket through the couscous, then place it in the centre of 4 plates. Top with the fish, spoon the salsa around and serve straight away.

SARDINE GRIGLIATE CON INSALATA DI PATATE

GRIDDLED SARDINES WITH WARM POTATO SALAD

The waters around Sardinia, where sardines are thought to have gained their name, are full of these beautiful fish, which are served on every local restaurant's menu.

~~~~~~~~~~~~~~~~~~~~~~~~~~~~~~~~~~~~~~~

Serves 4

1 LEMON	*For the salad*
8 FRESH SARDINES, GUTTED, CLEANED AND SCALED	1KG NEW POTATOES
	1 TEASPOON DIJON MUSTARD
8 FRESH ROSEMARY SPRIGS	1 TEASPOON RUNNY HONEY
OLIVE OIL	JUICE OF 1 LEMON
200G BABY PLUM TOMATOES ON THE VINE, CUT INTO SMALL BUNCHES	3 TABLESPOONS OLIVE OIL
	1 TABLESPOON FRESHLY CHOPPED CHIVES
SALT AND BLACK PEPPER TO TASTE	1 TABLESPOON FRESHLY CHOPPED OREGANO
GREEN SALAD TO SERVE	

First make the salad. Cook the potatoes in boiling salted water for 20-25 minutes until tender. Meanwhile, whisk together the mustard, honey and lemon juice in a large bowl. Slowly whisk in the olive oil, then add the herbs.

Drain the potatoes and cut any large ones in half.. Add them to the dressing and set aside to cool while you cook the sardines.

Cut the lemon into 8 slices, then cut each slice in half. Stuff 2 pieces into each fish cavity, along with a sprig of rosemary. Brush the outside of the fish with a little olive oil, then season with salt and pepper.

Preheat a griddle pan or barbecue and cook the sardines and tomatoes for 3 minutes on each side until the centre of the fish is cooked and the tomatoes have softened slightly.

Serve the fish with the warm potato salad, griddled tomatoes and a crisp green salad.

SARDINE GRIGLIATE CON INSALATA DI PATATE

COZZE ALL'ACQUA PAZZA

COZZE ALL'ACQUA PAZZA

STEAMED MUSSELS IN A BAG WITH CHILLI, WHITE WINE AND GARLIC

Mussels are fantastic value – great for a cheap feast. Just remember the golden rules: before cooking, discard any that have cracked shells or that don't close when tapped; and after cooking, discard any that haven't opened. Enjoy!

~~~~~~~~~~~~~~~~~~~~~~~~

Serves 4

1 GARLIC CLOVE, PEELED AND SLICED

1 RED CHILLI, DESEEDED AND FINELY SLICED

200ML PASSATA (SIEVED TOMATOES)

2 TABLESPOONS OLIVE OIL

SMALL GLASS OF WHITE WINE

2KG MUSSELS, CLEANED

SALT AND BLACK PEPPER TO TASTE

BREAD TO SERVE

Preheat the oven to 190°C/gas mark 5. Take 8 large sheets of foil roughly 40 x 40cm. Put 4 of them side by side and put the others on top.

Place the garlic, chilli, passata, olive oil and wine in a large bowl. Season with salt and pepper. Mix well, then add the mussels and stir to coat. Put equal amounts of the mussels on each double sheet of foil, placing them in a pile in the centre. (Don't worry about any liquid left in the bowl.)

Fold up the foil to enclose the mussels, leaving a little gap at one end. Pour any leftover sauce into the gap, then make a final fold to seal it.

Place the parcels on a baking tray and cook in the oven for 8-10 minutes.

I like to serve guests their own parcels so they get the experience of opening their own 'foodie bag' at the table. Make sure you have lots of bread at hand to mop up all the juices.

STUFATO DI PESCE ALLA SICILIANA

STUFATO DI PESCE ALLA SICILIANA

Sicilian Fish Stew

I have been cooking this recipe for years and very little has changed. It always brings back memories of when I lived in Sicily and would shop at the local fish market, then rush back home to cook up a large pot of this stew to enjoy with friends and a glass of chilled white wine. *Perfetto!*

~~~~~~~~~~~~~~~

Serves 4

3 TABLESPOONS OLIVE OIL

1 SMALL ONION, PEELED AND FINELY DICED

½ FENNEL BULB, FINELY DICED

2 CELERY STICKS, FINELY DICED

3 TOMATOES, DESEEDED AND DICED

PINCH OF DRIED CHILLI FLAKES

GLASS OF WHITE WINE

500ML FISH STOCK

A FEW FRESH PARSLEY SPRIGS

PINCH OF SAFFRON

300G FIRM WHITE FISH, CUT INTO 2CM CHUNKS

400G MUSSELS, CLEANED

400G CLAMS, CLEANED

8 LARGE RAW PRAWNS

ZEST OF ½ UNWAXED LEMON

1 TABLESPOON FRESHLY CHOPPED DILL

SALT AND BLACK PEPPER TO TASTE

Heat the oil in a large saucepan over a medium heat and fry the onion, fennel and celery for 3 minutes until soft. Add the tomatoes and chilli flakes and cook for another minute, then pour in the wine and allow to reduce by half.

Add the stock along with the parsley sprigs and saffron. Bring to a simmer and cook for 5 minutes.

Gently place the fish and shellfish in the pan and cover. Turn the heat down as low as possible and cook for 3 minutes.

Take the pan off the heat and leave to stand for 2 minutes, then season to taste and sprinkle with the lemon zest and dill. Serve immediately.

CAPESANTE CON PUREA DI PISELLI E PANE GRATTUGIATO

Scallops with Pea Purée and Spicy Pangrattato

This is a classic combination and perfect to cook when you want to impress friends without too much effort.

~~~~~~~~~~~~~~~~~~~~~~~~~~~~

Serves 4

12 HAND-DIVED SCALLOPS, CLEANED
1 TABLESPOON OLIVE OIL
JUICE OF ½ LEMON
SALT AND BLACK PEPPER TO TASTE
ROCKET AND WARM NEW POTATOES
  TO SERVE

For the pangrattato
½ CIABATTA LOAF

GOOD PINCH OF DRIED CHILLI FLAKES
ZEST OF 1 UNWAXED LEMON
2 TABLESPOONS OLIVE OIL

For the pea purée
250G FROZEN PEAS
SMALL BUNCH OF FRESH MINT
25G BUTTER
50ML DOUBLE CREAM

To make the pangrattato, place the ciabatta, chilli and lemon zest in a food processor or blender and blitz into fine to medium crumbs. Heat the oil in a frying pan and fry the crumbs for about 3 minutes until golden brown. Season with a pinch of salt and pepper, then set aside.

To make the purée, boil the peas in salted water for 3 minutes until tender. Drain, then blitz in a blender along with the mint, butter and cream until smooth. Season with salt and pepper. Return to the pan to keep warm.

Heat a large frying pan until smoking hot. Drizzle the scallops with oil and season with salt. Fry them on the salted side for 1 minute, then turn and cook the other side for 30-60 seconds, depending how thick the scallops are. Sprinkle with the lemon juice and transfer to a warm plate.

To serve, place a large spoonful of the pea purée on each plate, top with 3 scallops and a handful of rocket. Sprinkle over the pangrattato and finish with a drizzle of olive oil. Serve with the warm potatoes.

CAPESANTE CON PUREA DI PISELLI E PANE GRATTUGIATO

SIDES
&
SALADS

* * * * * * * * * * * * * * * *

SIDE DISHES AND SALADS ACCOMPANY every Italian meal, usually with the *secondo* course, where you would be served meat or fish. But like all other aspects of Italian cuisine, you can be sure that they will have been carefully thought out. We're not talking here about potatoes cooked in 101 different ways just to bulk out the meal. A true Italian dining table will have numerous side dishes that are just as important as the main course itself. Many will not contain starchy carbohydrates, especially if pasta has been eaten at the same meal. (Polenta and potatoes are served only when carbohydrates fail to appear elsewhere in the meal.) When this is the case, the focus will be on vegetables and pulses that are much lighter, while still being full of flavour.

Italy is blessed with an abundance of high-quality natural produce. The sun, together with the mountain waters in northern Italy and the nature of the soil in the south, miraculously combine to create perfect growing conditions for a wide range of vegetables and fruit. Olive and citrus groves abound, and together with vineyards, make the country one of the Mediterranean's leading food producers. Horticultural produce – most importantly tomatoes – is also widely cultivated, along with large quantities of mushrooms and truffles (in many regions pigs are still used to sniff them out), so there is no shortage of vegetables on offer.

Pickled vegetables are very popular, and many Italians like to do the preserving themselves as they don't like anyone messing about with their natural ingredients, especially adding chemicals. They will simply boil or grill the vegetable, then put it in a deep plate or jar and add olive oil and vinegar. One popular pickled vegetable dish, giardiniera, includes onions, carrots, celery and cauliflower, but many places in southern Italy, and particularly Sicily, also pickle aubergines and hot peppers.

Other side dish options include sliced fresh tomatoes topped with extra virgin olive oil, salt and basil, or fresh grilled vegetables drizzled with olive oil and vinegar and served at room temperature. These will be served with fresh bread and platters of meat – my mouth is salivating just thinking about it!

Most Italians will also grow some kind of herb, either in allotments and gardens or in pots on small balconies. I actually have a herb pot in my garden – there is nothing nicer than preparing a meal and cutting some herbs that you have grown, to add that extra flavour.

Salads in Italy tend to be pretty basic. Italians don't add a variety of ingredients to them as we do in the UK or USA. Salads (even large ones) are not normally served as a meal. They are there merely to provide a refreshing accompaniment to a meat or fish dish and will often just be

* * * * * * * * * * * * * * *

fresh leaves. The term 'salad dressing' strikes most Italians as very odd; our own term for it, *condire l'insalata*, which means 'to season a salad', is kind of dull in comparison to the many concoctions available to us elsewhere. Extra virgin olive oil is always the most essential ingredient, and is usually combined simply with white, red or balsamic vinegar, and sometimes lemon juice. When dressing a salad, always remember the golden rule: apply the dressing just a minute or so before serving it. If not, the vinegar or lemon will wilt the lettuce leaves. For this reason, any leftover dressed salad should be thrown out, so only dress the amount of salad you intend to eat immediately.

One ingredient in every Italian household and most houses around the world today will be olive oil. It's something that I, along with many other people, use every day. Italy is a net importer of olive oil and accounts for 21.5 per cent of the world's production. Major Italian producers are known as *città dell'olio*, or 'oil cities'. Noted centres for it include Lucca, Florence and Siena in Tuscany. However, the area of largest production is Puglia in the heel of Italy.

Olive oil is a fat obtained by grinding olives into a paste and then extracting the oil by mechanical means. Great care is taken in choosing the perfect ripened olives for a good extra virgin olive oil. Green olives are bitter and overripe olives produce a rancid taste.

The different names given to olive oil indicate the degree of processing the oil has undergone, as well as the quality of the oil itself. Extra virgin olive oil is produced simply by pressing the olives – no heating is involved, so it is described as cold-pressed. It has the strongest flavour with a minimum of bitterness. Virgin olive oil can involve the application of some heat and more pressing, while unlabelled oil may even involve the addition of chemicals to extract every last bit of oil from the olives. Virgin and regular oils have a milder taste then extra virgin, but they have a lower smoking point too, which means they are less likely to burn and are therefore better for cooking with. Extra virgin is generally used for dressing as its flavour is lost by heating. So if you are dressing your salad with olive oil, always make sure you use good-quality extra virgin. If you're cooking, though, remember to use just an ordinary olive oil.

As always, and as with most recipes in Italy, side dishes and salads tend to be about simple fresh ingredients. Not much is added so that the natural flavour of the individual ingredient speaks for itself. That's what I've aimed for with the side dishes and salads in this chapter – I hope you enjoy them.

ROME

LENTICCHIE A FUOCO LENTO
SLOW-COOKED LENTILS

Lentils are often eaten at New Year in Italy as they are believed to bring good fortune for the year ahead because of their coin-like shape. Whether they're lucky or not, you will always find them at my table on 31 December, but they are delicious all year round.

Serves 4

2 TABLESPOONS OLIVE OIL
25G BUTTER
1 ONION, PEELED AND FINELY CHOPPED
1 CARROT, PEELED AND FINELY CHOPPED
1 CELERY STICK, FINELY CHOPPED

200G ITALIAN GREEN LENTILS
300ML CHICKEN OR VEGETABLE STOCK
1 BAY LEAF
3 FRESH THYME SPRIGS
SALT AND BLACK PEPPER TO TASTE

Heat the oil in a sauté pan or frying pan over a medium to low heat and fry the butter, onion, carrot and celery for 10 minutes until they start to caramelise.

Rinse the lentils under cold water, then add them to the pan. Stir well to coat them in all the flavours, then add the stock and herbs. Cover and bring to a simmer.

Cook gently for 40 minutes, or until the lentils are tender, adding more stock if they become too dry. Remove the thyme sprigs and bay leaf, season and serve.

PATATE AL FORNO CON AGLIO, OLIO E ROSMARINO

Roasted Rosemary, Garlic and Olive Oil Potatoes

These are the Italian version of British roast potatoes, and one of the great things about them is that they create even less washing up because there's no need to boil the potatoes first. That also allows them to soak up even more flavour and get really crispy. These are so good they are not just for Sundays!

~~~~~~~~~~~~~~~~~~~~~~~~~

Serves 4

1KG FLOURY POTATOES

8 TABLESPOONS OLIVE OIL

1 GARLIC HEAD, CUT IN HALF HORIZONTALLY

6 FRESH ROSEMARY SPRIGS

SALT AND BLACK PEPPER TO TASTE

Preheat the oven to 200°C/gas mark 6.

Peel the potatoes and cut into 2cm cubes. Put the olive oil into a large roasting tray and place in the oven for 10 minutes until really hot.

Carefully tip the potatoes into the oil. Add the garlic, rosemary and a good pinch of salt and pepper. Using a large metal spoon, toss the ingredients together, then return the tray to the oven for 45 minutes, until the potatoes are tender and golden brown.

Serve with an extra sprinkling of sea salt. If you'd like them really garlicky, carefully remove the cloves of garlic from the halved heads and serve alongside the potatoes.

PATATE AL FORNO CON AGLIO, OLIO E ROSMARINO

CARPACCIO DI BARBABIETOLA

CARPACCIO DI BARBABIETOLA

Sliced Beetroot with Watercress and Walnut Pesto

If you are not a fan of beetroot, remember that it has many guises. It's not just our little friend in a jar that has been pickled to within an inch of its life; it can also be deliciously sweet when roasted, or beautifully earthy when eaten raw. If you hate the jarred stuff, try this recipe – it might just convert you.

Serves 4

2–3 LARGE BEETROOT
1 TABLESPOON OLIVE OIL
JUICE OF ½ LEMON
SMALL BUNCH OF WATERCRESS
25G WALNUT HALVES, ROUGHLY
  CHOPPED
SALT AND BLACK PEPPER TO TASTE

For the pesto
½ SMALL GARLIC CLOVE, PEELED
75G WATERCRESS
25G WALNUT HALVES
OLIVE OIL
40G FRESHLY GRATED PARMESAN
  CHEESE

Peel the beetroot, then thinly slice on a mandoline or by hand. Place the slices in a large bowl and drizzle over the olive oil and lemon juice with a pinch of salt. Toss everything together. (The acid will help 'cook' the beetroot so that it is not completely raw.) Leave for 1 hour.

To make the pesto, put the garlic, watercress and walnuts into a food processor or blender and blitz together. With the motor running, drizzle in the olive oil until the mixture has a consistency slightly thicker than double cream. Transfer the pesto to a bowl, stir in the Parmesan and season with black pepper.

Arrange the beetroot slices on a large plate. Scatter over the watercress leaves and chopped walnuts, then serve, drizzled with the delicious watercress pesto.

PATATE ALL'ORTOLANA

WARM NEW POTATOES, GREEN BEANS AND FENNEL WITH MUSTARD DRESSING

Sometimes mash or roast potatoes are a little too heavy, especially if the sun is shining. This is a great recipe and a perfect accompaniment to a simple steak or a roast chicken. What's even better about it is that it also includes two amazing vegetables, so you won't need to serve any additional side dishes.

~~~~~~

Serves 8

1KG NEW POTATOES

200G GREEN BEANS, TRIMMED AND
  HALVED

1 FENNEL BULB

ZEST OF 1 UNWAXED LEMON

SALT AND BLACK PEPPER TO TASTE

For the dressing

JUICE OF ½ LEMON

1 TABLESPOON RUNNY HONEY

1 TABLESPOON WHOLEGRAIN
  MUSTARD

3 TABLESPOONS OLIVE OIL

Gently boil the new potatoes in salted water for 20–25 minutes until tender. When done, add the beans and cook for 1 minute. Drain and transfer both potatoes and beans to a large bowl.

Finely slice the fennel bulb on a mandoline or by hand and add to the potatoes along with the lemon zest.

Mix all the dressing ingredients together, then pour it over the warm vegetables. The heat will help them to absorb the flavours of the dressing.

Season with salt and pepper and serve warm or cool.

PATATE ALL'ORTOLANA

ROME

CREMA DI POLENTA CON PARMIGIANO

CREAMY PARMESAN POLENTA

Polenta is a staple in many Italian households. It needs a helping hand with flavour, so making it with stock or milk, or even half and half, gives it a real boost. Also, a generous handful of Parmesan turns it from dull to extraordinary. It's true Italian comfort food, and any leftovers can be chilled, cut into slices and then grilled or fried. Really delicious and a great alternative to mashed potato.

Serves 6

400ML CHICKEN STOCK
350ML MILK
170G QUICK-COOK POLENTA
50G BUTTER

50G FRESHLY GRATED PARMESAN CHEESE
SALT AND BLACK PEPPER TO TASTE

Put the stock and milk into a large saucepan and bring to a simmer. Slowly pour in the polenta, whisking all the time. Continue whisking and boiling for 4-5 minutes (or according to the packet instructions) until thickened.

Remove from the heat and stir in the butter and Parmesan. Season to taste, adjust the consistency if needs be with a little more stock, and serve.

FAGIOLI CON ERBE E PANE GRATTUGIATO

HERBY BORLOTTI BEANS WITH OLIVE OIL BREADCRUMBS

People tend to think of beans and pulses as health foods with a mushy texture. But the best thing about them is that they are versatile and brilliant at taking on other flavours and textures. Here, with the simple addition of crispy breadcrumbs and herbs, they are transformed into little bubbles that really pack a punch.

~~~~~~~~~~~~~~~~~~~~~~~~~~~~~~~~~~~

Serves 4

1 TABLESPOON OLIVE OIL

2 GARLIC CLOVES, PEELED AND FINELY SLICED

2 FRESH ROSEMARY SPRIGS

2 X 400G TINS BORLOTTI BEANS, DRAINED AND RINSED

50ML CHICKEN STOCK

SALT AND BLACK PEPPER TO TASTE

For the breadcrumbs

50G STALE BREAD, IDEALLY CIABATTA

SMALL BUNCH OF FRESH PARSLEY

3 TABLESPOONS OLIVE OIL

ZEST OF 1 UNWAXED LEMON

SEA SALT

Heat the oil in a frying pan over a low heat and gently fry the garlic for 1 minute. Add the rosemary, beans and stock and bring to a simmer. Cook gently for 2–3 minutes until the beans are warmed through. Season to taste.

Place the bread and parsley in a food processor or blender and blitz until you have rough crumbs. Add the oil and lemon zest and pulse again.

Heat the oil in a frying pan over a low to medium heat and fry the crumbs until they start to turn crispy. (You will need to do this slowly to keep the bright green colour of the herb.) Sprinkle with salt.

Place the beans in a warm serving dish and serve sprinkled with the crispy breadcrumbs.

FAGIOLI CON ERBE E PANE GRATTUGIATO

INSALATA FANTASIA

ROCKET, PINE NUT AND POMEGRANATE SALAD

The pomegranate in this recipe gives a nod to the Arabic influences of Sicily's cooking. You can now buy little pots of pomegranate seeds in the supermarket, but I think half the fun is trying to extract the little jewels from the fruit. The best way to do this is to cut the fruit in half across the middle, hold each half upside down over a bowl and use a rolling pin to bash the skin gently so the seeds drop out. Alternatively, sit your kids down with cocktail sticks and let them extract the seeds one by one. It might just give you enough time to prepare the rest of the recipe!

~~~~~~~~~~

Serves 4

250G ROCKET LEAVES
1 BANANA SHALLOT, PEELED AND
   VERY THINLY SLICED
SEEDS FROM 1 POMEGRANATE
50G PINE NUTS
SALT AND BLACK PEPPER TO TASTE

For the dressing
1 TABLESPOON DIJON MUSTARD
2 TABLESPOONS RED WINE VINEGAR
4 TABLESPOONS OLIVE OIL
PINCH OF SUGAR (OPTIONAL)

Place the rocket in a large bowl with the shallot and pomegranate seeds.

Put the pine nuts in a dry frying pan and toast them lightly for 2-3 minutes until they are starting to turn golden brown. Tip them onto a chopping board and leave to cool.

To make the dressing, mix the mustard and vinegar together, then slowly whisk in the oil. Season with salt and pepper and a pinch of sugar if needed.

Dress and toss the salad, then scatter the toasted pine nuts over the top. Serve immediately.

INSALATA FANTASIA

VERDURE GRIGLIATE

Griddled Aubergine, Peppers and Courgettes Marinated in Garlic Oil

If you ever find vegetables a little boring, try the Italian way of preparing them. Lightly marinated in vinegar and olive oil, with added flavours such as garlic and herbs, they are perfect straight from the griddle, or eaten cold as part of a salad. The vinegar works really well and brings out the natural flavours of the vegetables. Trust me, I should know. I'm an Italian, after all!

~~~~~~~~~~~~~~~~~~~~

Serves 6

1 RED PEPPER, DESEEDED AND HALVED

1 YELLOW PEPPER, DESEEDED AND HALVED

2 COURGETTES

1 AUBERGINE

OLIVE OIL

2 TABLESPOONS WHITE WINE VINEGAR

1 GARLIC CLOVE, PEELED AND FINELY SLICED

2 TABLESPOONS CHOPPED FRESH DILL

SALT AND BLACK PEPPER TO TASTE

Heat a griddle pan on a high heat until really hot. Cut the peppers into large slices and place in a bowl. Cut the courgettes and aubergine into slices 1cm thick and add them to the bowl. Sprinkle with a little olive oil plus some salt and pepper and toss everything together.

Place the vegetables on the griddle (you might need to do this in batches) and allow them to char. (This will take a minute or so on each side.)

Return them to a bowl, drizzle with the vinegar, then add the garlic, a good glug of olive oil, the chopped dill and salt and pepper. Toss well.

Cover with cling film and marinate for 24 hours in the fridge, or serve immediately.

VERDURE AL FORNO CON TIMO E MIELE

Roasted Vegetables with Thyme and Honey

This is the easiest recipe in the world. I often cook it when I have lots of people over for supper, as I don't want loads of different pots and pans bubbling away on the hob. I can get everything ready in the roasting tray and just put it into the oven 1 hour before we want to eat. *Fantastico!*

~~~~~~~~~~~~~~~~~~~~~~~~~~~~~~~~

Serves 4–6

2 CARROTS	OLIVE OIL
2 BEETROOT	6 GARLIC CLOVES, UNPEELED
2 RED ONIONS	10 FRESH THYME SPRIGS
½ BUTTERNUT SQUASH	1 TABLESPOON HONEY
2 COURGETTES	SALT AND BLACK PEPPER TO TASTE

Preheat the oven to 180°C/gas mark 4.

Peel all the vegetable and cut them into large chunks and wedges – you want them all roughly the same size. Place them in a large roasting tray and drizzle with a generous glug of olive oil.

Use the flat side of a knife to gently squash the garlic cloves, but leave their skins on. Add these to the tray. Remove the thyme leaves from half the sprigs and scatter them over the vegetables. Place the remaining sprigs in the tray along with the honey.

Toss everything together, season and roast in the oven for 1 hour or until tender. Serve straight away.

ZUCCHINE FRITTE
FRIED CRISPY COURGETTES

There is something slightly more virtuous about eating courgette fries than the usual potato ones – after all, they are a green vegetable, so they must count as one of your five a day, right? Regardless of their slight naughtiness on health grounds, these are amazingly addictive and my chidren love them.

~~~~~~~~~~~~~~~~~~~~~~~~~~~~

Serves 4

5 LARGE COURGETTES
300ML COLD MILK
ABOUT 1 LITRE VEGETABLE OIL,
  FOR DEEP-FRYING

300G PLAIN FLOUR
SALT AND BLACK PEPPER TO TASTE

Cut all the courgettes into fine matchsticks. (You ideally need a mandoline with a thin 'chipping' attachment on it, but if not this can be done by hand.) Place them in a bowl and cover with the milk.

Heat a deep-fryer to 190°C or heat the oil in a deep pan until a cube of bread dropped in the oil sizzles and turns golden brown in 30 seconds.

Put the flour on a plate or in a shallow bowl and season with a pinch of salt and pepper..

Using a slotted spoon, remove the courgettes from the milk in batches, give them a good shake, then toss them in the seasoned flour. Carefully drop them into the hot oil and fry for 2–3 minutes until lightly golden.

Lift out with a slotted spoon and drain on kitchen paper. Sprinkle with salt and serve immediately.

ZUCCHINE FRITTE

BREAD
&
BISCUITS

* * * * * * * * * * * * * * *

IF YOU WERE TO ASK ME WHAT is my favourite smell of all time, it would have to be freshly baked breads or biscuits. There is nothing in the world like walking through the door and being greeted by that smell. My grandfather had a wood-burning oven in his garden, and many local people used to bring him simple ingredients, such as flour, yeast, salt and extra virgin olive oil, for him to make breads or pizza in exchange for some meats, fish or cheeses. I grew up making my own bread and, like him, have built a wood-burning oven in my garden too. I've done some experimenting, and I'm going to share some of my favourite results with you in this chapter.

Rarely is there an Italian meal that does not include bread. Ancient tools and ovens have given us proof that we have been making breads for thousands of years. As with many other foods, ancient Romans took the art of bread- making to a higher level (I know I'm biased but it is true). In addition to enhancing the milling techniques of wheat, the Romans were also the first to produce flour. Rome even opened a baking school in the 1st century AD.

Given this heritage, it's not surprising that Italians have very high standards for their bread. They quite often allow the dough to rise fully over the course of several hours, so it acquires a thin crust. Italians value the size of their loaves of bread too (no comments here, please!) because every family member needs to be properly nourished. They also prefer their bread to have a soft and moist interior, which is ideal for absorbing olive oil, vinegar, tomatoes and other toppings, but many of us in the south use just the crusty outside part.

When it comes to making bread, I would say that one of the most important parts of the process is kneading. Without getting too technical, you need to distribute the yeast equally so that the dough rises evenly. The texture you are looking for is quite tight and stretchy. Under-kneading will leave the dough soggy, while over-kneading (normally a problem only with food processors) will leave the bread with large holes in it. The best tools for kneading are your hands. A useful tip is to rub a little olive oil into them before you start kneading as it will help prevent the dough from sticking to your fingers.

Always remember to work your bread dough in a warm place, and make sure you have good weighing scales or accurate measuring jugs. It's also important that the water you use is at room temperature. In fact, all your ingredients, such as milk, eggs and butter, should be at room temperature.

Bread is one of the most variable of Italian foods: you'll find different flours or combinations of flours in different areas; some people use salt and

* * * * * * * * * * * * * * *

don't; some shape their breads into loaves, whereas others prefer circles, wheels, or even crosses; some brush their bread with oil, some dry it. And that's just a few of the variables... I'm sure you will have experienced, and most of you love, some of the more popular Italian breads, such as ciabatta, which originates from Liguria in northern Italy, focaccia from central Italy and, of course, the more rustic breads from my home town, Naples, in the south. Because of their flavour and popularity, it's these last ones I'm going to teach you how to make. Once you have the basics, you can be as creative with fillings and toppings as you wish: in fact, it gets to be addictive.

People often have the notion that baking is difficult, but it really isn't, I promise you, and the satisfaction you get is amazing. The next time you are shopping for breads or biscuits, have a look at the back of the wrapping and you will see that as many as 15 ingredients are listed. Fresh home baking actually needs no more than 3–5 ingredients and will cost you next to nothing.

I have chosen two of my all-time favourite *biscotti* (biscuits) for you to try. For me, nothing beats a good cup of coffee and one of these delicious crispy nibbles.

Cantuccini are baked twice (*bis-cotto* = twice cooked), so they are dry biscuits that are either dipped in sweet dessert wine (in Tuscany) or espresso (in Naples). What's brilliant about them is that they can be baked, kept for a week or two in a sealed container and still be perfect, so you could make a big batch and enjoy them for days.

My other choice is the famous amaretto biscotti. It is said that in the early 18th century, a Milanese bishop or cardinal surprised the town of Saronno with a visit. A young couple resident in the town welcomed him with an original confection: on the spur of the moment, they had combined sugar, egg whites and crushed apricot kernels or almonds to make delicious biscotti. The bishop absolutely loved them, and blessed the couple with a happy and lifelong marriage, resulting in the preservation of the secret recipe over many generations. Of course, today there are many variations but in my opinion, freshly baked amaretti con niccioline are the only way to go. One tip I would give you when making any kind of biscuit is to remember always to leave a little extra space between them as they will expand during baking.

I hope I have managed to convince you that baking is much easier than you think, and that you try these recipes. Baking things yourself really is hugely rewarding and looks extremely impressive when you serve your results to guests. You will be putting your own versions together in no time!

AMARETTI CON NOCCIOLINE

AMARETTI CON NOCCIOLINE

Soft Amaretti Biscuits with Crushed Hazelnuts

If you have tea with my family, you will definitely be served a freshly baked cake, but it will always, always be accompanied by freshly made amaretti biscuits. My recipe below produces the tastiest, yet easiest, amaretti you will ever make. They're wonderfully adaptable: if you store them in a sealed container for 3-4 days, they will become deliciously soft. Also try them crumbled over ice cream or fruit for dessert.

~~~~~~~~~~~~~~~~~~~~~~~~~~~~~~~~~~~~~~~

Makes about 30 biscuits

SALTED BUTTER FOR GREASING
4 EGG WHITES
350G CASTER SUGAR
350G GROUND ALMONDS

50ML AMARETTO LIQUEUR
80G CRUSHED HAZELNUTS
ICING SUGAR FOR DUSTING

Preheat the oven to 180°C/gas mark 4. Line a baking tray with greaseproof paper and lightly grease it with the butter.

Whisk the egg whites in a large, clean, dry bowl until stiff and firm. Gently mix in the sugar and almonds. Pour in the Amaretto liqueur and fold in carefully to make a smooth paste.

Gently fold in the crushed hazelnuts, then use a teaspoon to place small heaps of the mixture on the prepared tray, spacing them about 3cm apart to allow for expansion during cooking. Bake in the centre of the oven for 10-12 minutes until golden brown.

Enjoy the biscuits warm, or dry them on a rack until crisp and firm. Dust with a little icing sugar and serve with your favourite coffee.

CANTUCCINI ALLE MANDORLE

Classic Double-baked Biscuits with Almonds

While eating my fifth or sixth cantuccini, I often use the excuse that nuts are good for you. I love these crunchy finger-shaped biscuits – in fact, they are one of the most popular types in Italy and are always double-baked for extra crunch. You will often find them served with coffee or, if you are in northern Italy, with sweet dessert wine – but me, I'll have them with anything, including ice cream. Any excuse to have one more!

〜〜〜〜〜〜〜〜〜〜〜〜〜〜

Makes about 20 biscuits

150G WHOLE ALMONDS, SKINNED
280G WHITE FLOUR, TYPE 'OO'
150G CASTER SUGAR
1 TEASPOON BAKING POWDER
3 EGGS, BEATEN

1 TEASPOON VANILLA EXTRACT
ZEST OF 1 UNWAXED ORANGE
2 TABLESPOONS ORANGE LIQUEUR
ICING SUGAR FOR DUSTING

Preheat the oven to 180°C/gas mark 4 and line 2 baking trays with greaseproof paper.

Place the almonds in a small, dry frying pan over a medium heat and toast them for about 2 minutes, tossing occasionally untill they become lightly browned. Set aside.

Sift the flour into a large bowl. Add the sugar and baking powder. Stir in the toasted almonds with the eggs, vanilla extract, orange zest and liqueur to form a stiff dough.

Dust a work surface with icing sugar, divide the dough into 2 equal pieces and roll each piece into a sausage shape. Place them on the prepared baking trays and flatten slightly. Bake for 20 minutes in the middle of the oven until golden.

Remove the baked dough from the oven and lower the temperature to 150°C/gas mark 2.

Place the baked dough on a chopping board and, using a sharp knife, cut each piece diagonally into 1cm strips. Arrange them in a single layer on the baking trays and return to the oven for 5 minutes until golden brown.

Transfer the cantuccini to a wire rack to cool, then enjoy them with your favourite ice cream or a little glass of Amaretto liqueur.

FOCACCIA CON PANCETTA E CIPOLLE ROSSE

Focaccia Bread with Crispy Pancetta and Red Onions

Bacon and onion are already a winning combination, so adding them to home-made bread means that heaven has arrived. Please make sure that you use a strong white flour, and if you prefer fresh yeast, 10g will be more than enough for this recipe. This simple dimple-topped bread never fails to impress.

~~~~~~~~~~~~~~~~~~~~~~~~~~~~~~~~~~~~~

Serves 10

6 TABLESPOONS EXTRA VIRGIN OLIVE OIL, PLUS EXTRA FOR GREASING

500G STRONG WHITE FLOUR, PLUS EXTRA FOR DUSTING

1 TEASPOON FINE SALT

7G FAST-ACTION DRIED YEAST

300ML WARM WATER

2 TABLESPOONS SALTED BUTTER

250G DICED PANCETTA

1 LARGE RED ONION, PEELED AND CUT INTO 12 WEDGES

1 TABLESPOON COARSE SEA SALT

1 TEASPOON CRUSHED BLACK PEPPER

Brush a baking tray and the inside of a large bowl with oil.

Sift the flour and fine salt into a large bowl and stir in the yeast. Make a well in the centre and pour in 3 tablespoons of the oil plus the water. Mix together with a wooden spoon until all the ingredients are well combined.

Transfer the mixture to a lightly floured work surface and knead for 10 minutes until you have a smooth and elastic dough. Fold the edges underneath to form a smooth round ball and place it in the oiled bowl. Brush the top with a little more oil to prevent a crust from forming, then cover with cling film and leave to rise in a warm, draught-free place for 1 hour until nearly doubled in size.

Slide the risen dough onto the prepared baking tray and use your fingertips to make indentations in it, flattening it into a rectangular shape

FOCACCIA CON PANCETTA E CIPOLLE ROSSE

about 3cm thick. Brush with a little more oil, then cover with cling film and leave to rise again in a warm, draught-free place for 40 minutes.

Preheat the oven to 220°C/gas mark 7.

Melt the butter in a pan and fry the pancetta until crispy. Set aside, then fry the onion wedges in a little oil until starting to colour on one side. Scatter them both over the risen dough. Drizzle 3 tablespoons of oil all over, then sprinkle with the coarse sea salt and crushed black pepper.

Bake in the middle of the oven for 20 minutes until golden and cooked through. Cool on a wire rack so that the bottom does not become soggy..

Serve warm.

PANE RUSTICO

Rustic Tuscan-style Bread

Similar to a baguette, only shorter and fatter, this type of bread is popular throughout Italy as an everyday loaf. It especially suits rich dishes, such as hearty stews and casseroles, but in all honesty you can use it for anything.

~~~~~~~~~~~~~~~~~~~~~~~~~~~

Makes 2 long loaves

EXTRA VIRGIN OLIVE OIL FOR BRUSHING

500G STRONG WHITE FLOUR

½ TEASPOON SEA SALT

1 TEASPOON CASTER SUGAR

7G FAST-ACTION DRIED YEAST

300ML WARM WATER

Brush the inside of a large bowl with oil. Sift the flour into another large bowl. Add the salt, sugar and yeast and mix well with a wooden spoon. Pour in the water and mix again until all the ingredients come together, then transfer the mixture to a floured work surface and knead by hand for about 15 minutes, until the dough becomes smooth and silky.

Place the dough in the oiled bowl, cover with cling film and leave to rise in a warm, draught-free place for 2 hours until doubled in size.

Divide the dough into half and flatten each piece to a thickness of about 2.5cm. Then, as if making a Swiss roll, start rolling up the dough loosely until you have something that looks like a loaf.

Place the loaves on a lightly floured baking tray and cover with a damp cloth. Leave to rest for another hour, until doubled in volume.

Preheat the oven to 180°C/gas mark 4. When it reaches temperature, spray the sides of it with cold water or place a dish of water in the bottom. The steam created will give colour and a nice crust.

Use a sharp knife to gently score each loaf straight down the middle, then bake them for 20 minutes, until they are golden. Serve while they are still warm.

FOCACCIA FARCITA

FOCACCIA FARCITA

ROLLED FOCACCIA STUFFED WITH MOZZARELLA AND TOMATOES

I absolutely love this bread; it's almost a meal in itself, and with all the flavours I've put inside, could almost pass for a pizza. You can be as creative as you like and add almost anything (spinach and olives are a good option), but the melted cheese with the tomatoes is a match made in heaven. Eat the bread warm or at room temperature with any choice of starters and your guests will be hugely impressed. It's also great to take with you in your lunch-box or on a picnic.

～～～～～～～～～～～～～～～～～～

Makes 1 long loaf

2 TABLESPOONS EXTRA VIRGIN OLIVE OIL, PLUS EXTRA FOR BRUSHING

350G STRONG WHITE FLOUR, PLUS EXTRA FOR DUSTING

1 TEASPOON SALT

½ TEASPOON CASTER SUGAR

5G FAST-ACTION DRIED YEAST

200ML WARM WATER

1 TABLESPOON FRESH ROSEMARY LEAVES

For the filling

2 MOZZARELLA BALLS, DRAINED AND CUT INTO SMALL CUBES

50G FRESHLY GRATED PARMESAN CHEESE

150G SUN-DRIED TOMATOES IN OIL, DRAINED

1 TEASPOON FRESHLY GROUND BLACK PEPPER

1 GARLIC CLOVE, PEELED AND CRUSHED

Brush a baking tray and the inside of a large bowl with oil.

Mix the flour, salt, sugar and yeast in another large clean bowl and make a well in the centre. Pour in the water and mix with your fingers until you have a soft sticky dough.

Transfer the dough to a lightly floured work surface and knead for about 10 minutes until smooth and elastic. Shape into a ball and place in the oiled bowl. Brush the top with a little oil, cover with cling film and leave to rise in a warm, draught-free place for 1 hour.

Transfer the risen dough to a lightly floured work surface and roll into a rectangular shape about 30 x 25cm. Cover with cling film and leave to rest for 5 minutes.

Place the ingredients for the filling in a large bowl and mix to combine. Scatter the filling over the rested dough, leaving a 1cm clear margin all around the edge.

Starting from the shorter side, roll up the dough like a Swiss roll, then tuck the ends under to seal. Place the roll, seam down, on the oiled baking tray. Cover with cling film and leave to rest in a warm, draught-free place for 30 minutes.

Preheat the oven to 200°C/gas mark 6.

Brush the roll with the 2 tablespoons of olive oil and use a skewer to prick holes all over it. Sprinkle with the rosemary leaves.

Bake in the middle of the oven for 35 minutes until golden, then transfer to a wire rack to cool.

Slice and serve warm with a little salad of your choice.

PANINI
Breakfast Bread Rolls

Although these are called breakfast rolls, you can eat them at any time with either sweet or savoury fillings. *Panini* translates simply as 'rolls', but the form that has become widely recognised in the UK is soft and rectangular with grill marks. The recipe below produces something smaller, more akin to bridge rolls. Served warm, they are simply delicious! You can play around with the toppings, perhaps adding black sesame seeds or poppy seeds for a different finish.

~~~~~~~~~~~~~~~~~~~~~~~~~

Makes 8 rolls

7G FAST-ACTION DRIED YEAST

250ML WARM FULL-FAT MILK

500G STRONG WHITE FLOUR, PLUS
   EXTRA FOR DUSTING

30G CASTER SUGAR

1·TEASPOON FINE SALT

100G SOFT UNSALTED BUTTER

1 EGG, BEATEN

Put the yeast into a large bowl, add 3 tablespoons of the milk and stir until dissolved. Add 30g of the flour and a teaspoon of the sugar, then mix and knead until you have a small piece of dough of even consistency. Place it in a floured bowl, cut a cross on the top and let it stand in a warm, draught-free place for 30 minutes.

Sift the remaining flour onto the work surface and add the salt and remaining sugar. Make a well in the centre and mix in the remaining milk. Incorporate the dough prepared earlier, then add the soft butter in small pieces. Knead vigorously until the dough starts to come away from your hands and the work surface more easily.

Shape the dough into a ball and put into a clean floured bowl. Cut a cross on the top, cover with a tea towel and let it rest in a warm, draught-free place for 2 hours until doubled in volume.

Line a baking sheet with baking paper and lightly dust it with flour.

Divide the dough into 8 equal pieces and work each of these into a regular smooth ball on a floured work surface. Arrange them on the prepared baking sheet, cover with a tea towel and leave to rise again for 30 minutes.

Preheat the oven to 220°C/gas mark 7.

Brush the surface of each roll with the beaten egg (this will give them a lovely sheen). Bake in the middle of the oven for 20 minutes until beautifully golden.

Set the panini aside to cool before serving.

PANINI

CIABATTA CLASSICA
CLASSIC CIABATTA BREAD

This recipe really is quite simple and so worth it. With just a little bit of effort, you can create one of the most famous Italian breads in your own home. It's ideal dipped into a good-quality extra virgin olive oil.

~~~~~~~~~~~~~~~~~~~~~~~~~~~~~~~~

Makes 4 small loaves

450G STRONG WHITE FLOUR, PLUS
  EXTRA FOR DUSTING
10G FRESH YEAST
340ML WARM WATER
50ML EXTRA VIRGIN OLIVE OIL, PLUS
  EXTRA FOR GREASING
1 TEASPOON SALT

For the starter (biga)
350G STRONG WHITE FLOUR
180ML WARM WATER
5G FRESH YEAST

First prepare the starter, or *biga*. Place all the ingredients for it in a large bowl and mix by hand for 5 minutes to form a rough dough. Cover with cling film and leave to rest in a warm, draught-free place for 20 hours.

To make the dough, place the flour in a large bowl and rub in the yeast. Scoop out the starter that you previously prepared and place in the bowl with the flour and yeast. Pour in the water and oil, add the salt and mix until well combined. Transfer the dough to a lightly floured work surface and knead for 8 minutes until you have a smooth ball.

Brush the inside of a clean bowl with oil and place the dough in it. Cover with cling film and leave to rise in a warm, draught-free place for 1–1½ hours until bubbly and light.

Place the risen dough on a floured work surface and sprinkle a little flour on top. Gently press down with your fingers to flatten it, then cut it into 4 equal strips. Take one strip of dough, fold one short side of it into the middle, then bring the other side over to meet it. Press down to seal. Finally, fold in half lengthways and press to seal the edges. Repeat this process with the remaining strips of dough.

Cover a baking sheet with a tea towel and sprinkle it with flour. Place the 4 pieces of dough on the tea towel, cover with another tea towel and leave to rest in a warm, draught-free place for 40 minutes.

Preheat the oven to 220°C/gas mark 7.

Flour a baking tray. Pick up 1 ciabatta at a time, turn it over and lay it on the prepared tray. Gently stretch the dough lengthways to create the characteristic slipper shape.

Spray the inside of the oven with water or place a dish of water in the bottom. Bake the ciabatta on the middle shelf for 20 minutes until beautifully golden.

Serve warm to accompany any meal.

AMALFI

PAGNOTTA CON FINOCCHIETTO

PAGNOTTA CON FINOCCHIETTO

Southern Italian Loaf Encrusted with Fennel Seeds

I can't think of this bread without remembering Naples, when the baking smells seemed to fill the streets and my friends and I would use all our charm to persuade the baker to give us a piece or two. Although this seems like a basic rustic bread, it will surprise you with the flavour it delivers. This is the bread I make if I want a loaf that lasts. Instead of the fennel seeds you can leave it plain, or try sesame or poppy seeds if you prefer.

~~~~~~

Makes 1 large loaf

OLIVE OIL FOR BRUSHING

470G STRONG WHITE FLOUR

1 TEASPOON SALT, PLUS A PINCH FOR THE TOPPING

1 TABLESPOON CASTER SUGAR

10G FAST-ACTION DRIED YEAST

1 TABLESPOON FENNEL SEEDS, CRUSHED

300ML WARM WATER

40G SALTED BUTTER, MELTED

1 EGG WHITE

Brush a baking tray and the inside of a large bowl with oil.

Sift the flour into a large clean bowl. Mix in the salt, sugar and yeast and make a well in the centre. Sprinkle in about a third of the fennel seeds, then add the water and butter. Mix with your fingertips until you have a soft dough.

Place the dough on a lightly floured work surface and knead for 10 minutes until smooth and elastic. Shape it into a ball and place in the oiled bowl. Cover with cling film and leave it to rise in a warm, draught-free place for 1 hour.

Turn the risen dough onto a floured work surface and punch down. Shape into a fat oval and place on the oiled baking tray. Brush the top with a little oil and cover with cling film. Leave it to rise in a warm, draught-free place for 40 minutes.

Preheat the oven to 220°C/gas mark 7.

Mix the egg white with the pinch of salt in a small bowl. Brush this over the top of the loaf and sprinkle with the remaining fennel seeds. Use a sharp knife to make a cut along its length.

Bake in the middle of the oven for 20 minutes, then lower the temperature to 180°C/gas mark 4 and continue to bake for a further 10 minutes.

Transfer to a wire rack to cool and serve warm with your favourite selection of grilled marinated vegetables.

SCHIACCIATA CON AGLIO E PREZZEMOLO

FLATBREAD WITH GARLIC AND PARSLEY

Any garlic bread is amazing in flavour but you just have to try this one...the addition of fresh parsley makes it stunning. This is a perfect antipasti bread, especially if you have lots of starter dishes with many different flavours. You can substitute the parsley with fresh mint leaves but if you ask me, parsley works brilliantly. My mother used to give my sister Marcella and me this schiacciata for our school packed lunch. Delicious with a little soft cheese on the side!

~~~~~~~~~~~~~~~~~~~~~~~

Makes 6 flatbreads

3 TABLESPOONS EXTRA VIRGIN OLIVE OIL, PLUS EXTRA FOR BRUSHING
500G STRONG WHITE FLOUR
2 TEASPOONS SEA SALT
1 TEASPOON CASTER SUGAR
5G FAST-ACTION DRIED YEAST
350ML WARM WATER

For the topping
5 GARLIC CLOVES, PEELED AND CHOPPED
3 TABLESPOONS FRESHLY CHOPPED FLAT LEAF PARSLEY
1 TEASPOON SEA SALT

Brush 2 baking trays and the inside of a large bowl with oil. Dust the trays with flour.

Sift the flour into a large clean bowl. Add the salt, sugar and yeast and mix everything together. Make a well in the centre and pour in 2 tablespoons of the oil plus the water. Mix with a wooden spoon until a rough dough forms, then transfer to a floured surface and knead by hand for about 10 minutes until smooth and elastic.

Place the dough in the oiled bowl, cover with cling film and leave to rise in a warm, draught-free place for about 2 hours until it has at least doubled in size.

Transfer the dough to a lightly floured surface and divide into 6 equal pieces, forming each one into an oval shape about 15cm long. Place the pieces on the 2 baking trays to rest for 20–30 minutes.

Taking each dough piece in turn, flatten them with your fingertips to a thickness of 1–1.5cm and about 20cm long and 10cm wide. Return to the baking trays, brush with the remaining tablespoon of olive oil and sprinkle with the garlic, parsley and salt.

Use a sharp knife or pizza cutter to make 3 diagonal slashes in the top of each bread. Cover with a tea towel and leave to rise in a warm, draught-free place for 1 hour.

Preheat the oven to 180°C/gas mark 4.

Widen the cuts in the risen breads with your fingertips so that, once baked, they will be easier to tear and share.

Bake for 13–15 minutes until golden brown, then place on a wire rack to cool slightly.

Serve warm with your favourite selection of cured hams and salami.

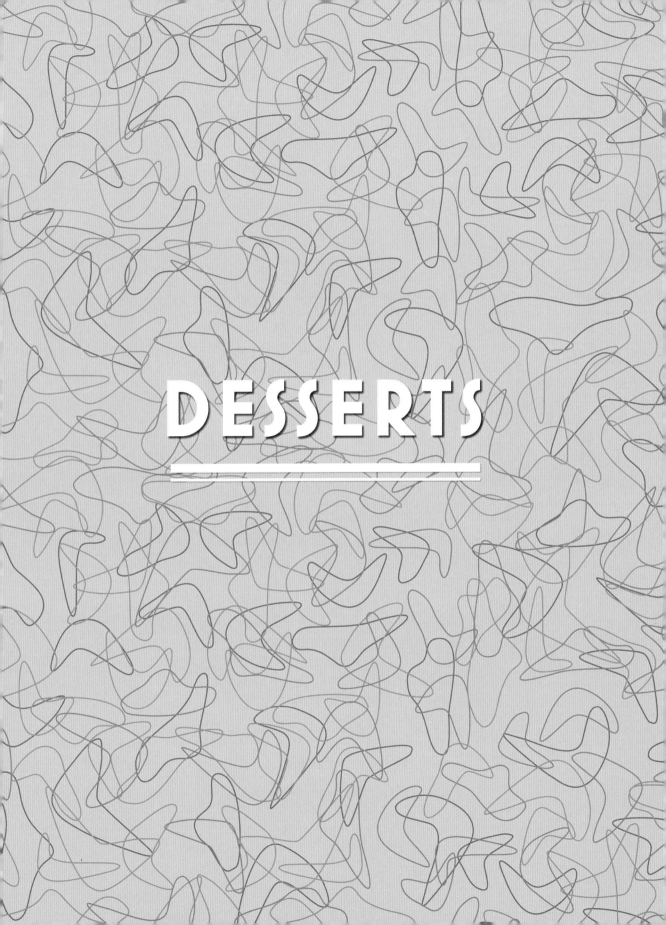

DESSERTS

* * * * * * * * * * * * * * * *

MY FAMILY LOVE DESSERTS so I am always trying to come up with
something new, and I have chosen some of our current favourites for
this chapter. The Panna Cotta al Baileys (see page 274) is fantastic for a
dinner party as you can make it well in advance. What I really love, though,
is ice cream. I reckon my favourite dessert of all time is *affogato*, a home-
made vanilla ice cream topped with a cup of espresso coffee – heaven. I
challenge anyone to taste and not love real Italian ice cream. In Naples
the combinations on offer are amazing – so much so that when my family
go to a *gelateria* there, we often choose small scoops of lots of different
flavours as we simply can't decide what to have. The colours alone make
you want to smile.

Many people believe that Marco Polo brought ice cream to Italy from
China but Roman emperors were known to have enjoyed similar desserts
centuries before him. Although Italy may not have originally created
frozen desserts, it has played an important role in creating ice cream
and bringing it to Europe.

It is said that the Arabs introduced sorbet to southern Italy. They would
use fruit juices and mountain snow to make *sharbat* (a frozen sherbet or
sorbet). The closest approximation to this is *granita*, a Sicilian dessert
made of coarse grated ice, sugar and flavourings. But it would take a
few centuries before milk or cream began to be added to convert these
sorbets into true ice cream. And, just as with pizza, it is the Neapolitans
who are credited with doing it. Once dairy products had been introduced,
each nationality put its own stamp on ice cream, with Italy creating the
flavour explosion known as *gelato*.

The differences between ice cream and Italian gelato are minimal but
still make a massive difference in terms of flavour and texture. Gelato is
made with milk (sometimes skimmed) as opposed to cream, which gives
it a much lower fat content and allows its flavours to really stand out
compared to the more blended flavours of ice cream. The flavour of gelato
is also helped by the fact that it has less air whipped into it than ice cream,
making it much denser. Even the consistency is different – gelato is softer,
more along the lines of soft-serve ice cream.

One of my favourite granita, or sorbet, options has to be with lemons
from Sorrento. These are harvested all year round, with the peak season
being from spring to late autumn. They were once so highly regarded that
they used to be sold individually and could only be handled by women who
had trimmed nails and wore cotton gloves.

The Sorrento lemon is large and oval in shape, with tapered ends and
quite a thick peel that is highly fragrant. Used for their juice and peel,

TORRE DEL GRECO

* * * * * * * * * * * * * * * *

these lemons are one of the richest sources of vitamin C, and in November 2000 they earned their own IGP (Protected Geographical Indication), which is similar to the prestigious AOC designation for cheeses. Sorrento lemon groves are said to help the environment by preserving the stability of the soil. Approximately 60 per cent of their yield is used to make the Italian liqueur limoncello (purists say that Sorrento lemons are the only ones to be used for this purpose). After a heavy meal, this strong refreshing liqueur is wonderful both in taste and for its ability to aid digestion. The more bitter Amaro is another after-meal option, but many people prefer to choose a sweet dessert wine.

Dessert wines are a great way to end a meal. In fact, in Italy desserts are always served with dessert wine rather than coffee or tea. Italians generally linger at the table after a meal, taking time to chat, nibble sweets or nuts, and relax after normally a very filling long lunch or dinner, and the wines are an integral part of this process. A general rule is that the wine should be sweeter than the food it is served with. White dessert wines are generally served chilled but not very cold, while red dessert wines are served at room temperature or very slightly chilled.

There are many varieties of dessert wine in Italy. In fact, there's an Italian dessert wine to suit every cheese, every pudding and every mood. My three personal favourites are Vin Santo (literally 'holy wine'), an amber-coloured Tuscan wine made from dried grapes; Moscato d'Asti, a sweet white dessert wine from Piedmont, made from the Moscato Bianco grape; and Brachetto d'Acqui, a red dessert wine produced in the provinces of Asti and Alessandria and blended with Aleatico and Moscato Nero grapes. However, if you are ever in Italy I urge you to try a dessert wine from whichever region you're in – you won't be disappointed.

This really is a brilliant way to end a meal and I highly recommend it.

LA CAPRESE DI ZIA RITA

My Auntie Rita's Pistachio and Chocolate Cake

Sometimes my Auntie Rita made this cake for me and my sister as an after-school treat. It's great for teatime, perfect as a dessert, and amazing if you have any gluten-free friends coming round.

~~~~~~~~~~~~~~~~~~~~~

Serves 8

80G SHELLED PISTACHIO NUTS

100G SALTED BUTTER, PLUS EXTRA
  FOR GREASING

250G GOOD-QUALITY DARK
  CHOCOLATE (70% COCOA SOLIDS)

4 EGGS, SEPARATED

160G ICING SUGAR, PLUS EXTRA FOR
  DUSTING

150G GROUND ALMONDS

Put the pistachios in a heatproof bowl, cover with boiling water and leave to soak for 3 minutes. Drain and peel off the skin, then roughly chop.

Preheat the oven to 180°C/gas mark 4 and grease a 23cm shallow, loose-bottomed cake tin.

Melt the butter and chocolate in a large bowl set over a pan of simmering water (the bowl must not actually touch the water). In a separate large bowl, whisk the egg yolks and icing sugar until fluffy and pale in colour. In another large, dry bowl, whisk the egg whites until stiff.

Pour the melted chocolate into the yolk mixture and stir well. Mix in the almonds and chopped pistachios, then gently fold in the egg whites with a metal spoon.

Pour the mixture into the prepared tin and bake in the middle of the oven for 30 minutes until a skewer inserted in the centre comes out clean.

Let the cake rest for 10 minutes, then unmould onto a plate. Slice and serve at room temperature, dusted with icing sugar,. A tablespoon of mascarpone or double cream and a little glass of Vin Santo are lovely accompaniments.

CREMA DI LIMONI E LIMONCELLO

LEMON AND LIMONCELLO MOUSSE

The Amalfi coastline is one of the most stunning in Italy and its natural beauty brings many tourists to the area. The area's other claim to fame is its production of lemons. The coastal cliffs are dotted with terraces of lemon trees, some of them bearing fruit the size of rugby balls. The locals use these versatile fruits to their full potential: many lemon grove owners make and sell bottles of limoncello, and street vendors sell refreshing lemon sorbet.

Serves 4–6

250G MASCARPONE CHEESE

ZEST OF 2 AMALFI OR UNWAXED LEMONS

3 TABLESPOONS LIMONCELLO LIQUEUR

3 EGG WHITES

50G CASTER SUGAR

8 AMARETTI BISCUITS

Mix together the mascarpone, lemon zest and limoncello.

Whisk the egg whites to stiff peaks, then whisk in the caster sugar. Fold half of it through the mascarpone mixture, then fold in the remaining half. This will help keep it light and fluffy.

Spoon the mixture into glasses and eat straight away if you like a fairly liquid texture. Alternatively, set in the fridge for 30 minutes or even overnight. Before serving, crumble the amaretti biscuits over the top.

CREMA DI LIMONI E LIMONCELLO

GELATO AL LIMONCELLO

GELATO AL LIMONCELLO

LIMONCELLO ICE CREAM

Many people enjoy lemon sorbet but miss the creamy texture of ice cream, so I have created a limoncello ice cream. You still get the refreshing lemon flavour, with a little extra kick from the limoncello liqueur, but the texture is creamier, allowing you to enjoy a *gelato*-like consistency without the usual sweetness. The result feels more like a dessert than a sorbet, yet still leaves your palate feeling cleansed.

~~~~~~~~~~~~~~~~~~~~~~~~~~

Serves 6

2 UNWAXED LEMONS

6 EGG YOLKS

50ML FRESHLY SQUEEZED LEMON
 JUICE

100G CASTER SUGAR

30ML LIMONCELLO LIQUEUR

500ML DOUBLE CREAM, LIGHTLY
 WHIPPED

Finely grate the skin of the lemons and set aside.

Place the egg yolks in a heatproof bowl set over a pan of steaming water off the heat. Whisk until light and fluffy and increased in volume. Add the lemon juice, sugar, grated lemon skin and limoncello and continue whisking until thick and pale. Set aside and allow to cool.

Gently fold the cream into the limoncello mixture. Pour into an ice cream machine and churn according to the manufacturer's instructions. Alternatively, pour into a freezerproof container, cover and freeze for 2 hours until crystals start to form. Remove from the freezer, beat well with a fork or electric beater and freeze again for 1 hour. Repeat the beating and freezing twice more at hourly intervals.

Cover the finished ice cream with baking paper and a lid and freeze until solid. Allow to soften slightly before serving,

GELATO ALLA FRAGOLA

Easy Strawberry Ice Cream

This is a really easy ice cream recipe. One of my friends was coming over one afternoon to watch a football match on TV and I asked him what he wanted to eat as a snack. For some reason he really fancied strawberry ice cream. I didn't have any fresh strawberries so I tried it with strawberry jam and it worked brilliantly. Use cherry or raspberry jam if you prefer – they all work really well.

Serves 6

250G MASCARPONE CHEESE
200ML FULL-FAT MILK
100G CASTER SUGAR

3 TABLESPOONS AMARETTO LIQUEUR
1 X 300G JAR GOOD-QUALITY
STRAWBERRY JAM

Put the mascarpone, milk, sugar and Amaretto in a food processor. Blitz until all the ingredients are well combined.

Pour into an ice cream machine and churn according to the manufacturer's instructions. Alternatively, pour into a freezerproof container , cover and freeze for 2 hours until crystals start to form. Remove from the freezer, beat well with a fork or electric beater and freeze again for 1 hour. Repeat the beating and freezing once more, then return to the freezer for a further 2 hours.

Stir in the strawberry jam at the end before the mixture is frozen for the final time.

Cover the finished ice cream with baking paper and a lid. The end result is a soft-textured ice cream, ready to be served straight from the freezer.

GELATO ALLA FRAGOLA

SORBETTO AL LIMONE

Fresh Lemon and Lime Sorbet

As I've mentioned in the main introduction, the lemons near where I live in southetn Italy are truly amazing, but any good-quality lemon will make this recipe fantastic. If you don't have a sweet tooth and prefer more of a tangy dessert, this is definitely the choice for you. It could also be used as a palate cleanser between courses.

~~~~~~~~~~~~~~~~~~~~

Serves 6

2 UNWAXED LIMES
100G CASTER SUGAR

350ML FRESHLY SQUEEZED LEMON JUICE

Finely grate the skin of the limes and set aside.

Squeeze the juice from the limes and place in a medium saucepan with 1 litre of cold water. Add the sugar and half the lime zest and simmer for 5 minutes until the sugar has dissolved, stirring occasionally with a wooden spoon. Remove from the heat, add the lemon juice and mix well. Set aside to cool.

Pourthe lemon mixture into an ice cream machine and churn according to the manufacturer's instructions. Alternatively, pour it into a shallow freezerproof container, cover and freeze for 2 hours until crystals start to form around the edges. Remove from the freezer, stir vigorously with a fork and return to the freezer for 20 minutes.

Repeat this process every 20 minutes over the next few hours until there is no liquid left in the container and the mixture is just broken ice crystals.

Once ready, allow the sorbetto to soften slightly so it is easier to scoop.

Serve in tall glasses and decorate with the remaining lime zest on top.

GELATO AL CIOCCOLATO
Chocolate and Cinnamon Ice Cream

My son Rocco doesn't really like drinking milk, so I am always trying to think of different ways I can get a bit of calcium into him. For dessert you can't get better than ice cream and, miraculously, I have never had a no from him on this one! You can leave out the cinnamon if you prefer, or even use fresh mint instead – both work well.

~~~~~~~~~~~~~~~~~~~~~~~~~~~~

Serves 6

500ML FULL-FAT MILK
250G GOOD-QUALITY DARK
   CHOCOLATE (70% COCOA SOLIDS),
   CUT INTO PIECES
3 CINNAMON STICKS

200G CASTER SUGAR
1 TEASPOON GROUND CINNAMON
4 EGG YOLKS
500ML DOUBLE CREAM

Heat the milk, chocolate and cinnamon in a heavy-based saucepan over a low heat for 15 minutes, stirring occasionally with a wooden spoon. Do not allow to boil. Once the chocolate has melted, discard the cinnamon sticks and set the pan aside.

Mix the sugar and ground cinnamon in a large heatproof bowl. Add the egg yolks and place the bowl over a pan of simmering water. Whisk until the mixture is thick and pale, then gradually whisk in the chocolate mixture. Continue whisking for 6 minutes, until light and fluffy. Set aside to cool for 1 hour.

Stir the cream into the chocolate mixture. Pour into an ice cream machine and churn according to the manufacturer's instructions. Alternatively, pour into a freezerproof container, cover and freeze for 2 hours until crystals start to form. Remove from the freezer, beat well with a fork or electric beater until smooth and freeze again for 1 hour. Repeat the beating and freezing twice more at hourly intervals.

Cover the finished ice cream with baking paper and a lid and freeze until solid. Allow to soften slightly before serving..

TORTINE AL CIOCCOLATO

CHOCOLATE CUPCAKES

One of my favourite chocolates is Ferrero Rocher, and I've tried so often to incorporate it in desserts, but it's never really worked … until now. Not only are these cupcakes to die for, they are also the quickest, easiest you'll ever make.

~~~~~~~~~~~~~~~~~~~~~~~~~~~~~~

Makes 12 cupcakes

8 FERRERO ROCHER CHOCOLATES, COLD FROM THE FRIDGE

85G UNSALTED BUTTER, AT ROOM TEMPERATURE

125G CASTER SUGAR

2 EGGS

100G NATURAL YOGHURT

115G SELF-RAISING FLOUR, SIFTED

For the topping

4 TABLESPOONS NUTELLA CHOCOLATE SPREAD

4 TABLESPOONS CRUSHED HAZELNUTS

Preheat the oven to 160°C/gas mark 3. Line a baking tray with 12 paper cupcake cases.

Remove the Ferrero Rocher wrappers and place the chocolates in a small bag. Crush gently with a rolling pin and set aside.

Place all the remaining ingredients (except those for the topping) in a large bowl and whisk vigorously until fully combined. Gently stir in the crushed chocolates with a flexible spatula, then use a tablespoon to divide the mixture equally between the paper cases.

Bake for 25 minutes until the cupcakes are well risen and springy in the centre, or until a skewer inserted into the centre comes out clean. Transfer to a wire rack and leave to cool for 30 minutes.

Using the back of a teaspoon, spread the Nutella over the top of each cupcake and sprinkle the chopped hazelnuts on top.

Serve with a little cup of espresso coffee.

PANNA COTTA AL BAILEYS

BAILEYS PANNA COTTA

Like most great concoctions, this dessert was created by chance when my wife bought a bottle of Baileys liqueur for one of our dinner guests. I thought I'd try it in the panna cotta I was making... All I can say is 'Wow'!

〜〜〜〜〜〜〜〜〜〜〜〜〜〜〜〜

Serves 6

175G GRANULATED SUGAR

600ML SEMI-SKIMMED MILK

2 TEASPOONS VANILLA EXTRACT

4 EGGS, PLUS 4 EGG YOLKS

60G CASTER SUGAR

100ML BAILEYS LIQUEUR

Place the granulated sugar in a large saucepan over a low heat, slowly stirring with a wooden spoon until the sugar has dissolved. Bring to the boil and bubble for 2-3 minutes until the mixture turns a pale caramel colour. Pour it into 6 ramekins, tilting them so that the caramel coats the bottom and halfway up the sides. Set aside to cool.

Preheat the oven to 160°C/gas mark 3.

Pour the milk into a saucepan, add the vanilla extract and heat until almost boiling. Set aside to cool slightly.

Beat the eggs, egg yolks and caster sugar together in a large bowl. Pour into the milk along with the Baileys and whisk together.

Divide the milk mixture between the ramekins and place them in a roasting tin. Pour in enough cold water to come halfway up the side of the dishes, then place in the oven for 25 minutes until set, or until a skewer inserted into the centre comes out clean. Remove the ramekins from the roasting tin and set aside to cool.

When ready to serve, run a sharp knife around the edge of each panna cotta, place a small plate over the top and flip over.

Serve the panna cotta with the caramel poured around it.

PANNA COTTA AL BAILEYS

PASTIERA

RASPBERRY AND ORANGE BAKED CHEESECAKE

This is quite an old-fashioned recipe from my home patch, and I must admit, I wasn't a huge fan of it when growing up (probably because of all the fruit and lack of chocolate), but now I really appreciate all the flavours and how well they work together. My grandfather, Giovanni, used to make this at Easter and now I carry on the tradition.

~~~~~~~~~~~~~~~~~~~~~~~~~~~~~~~~

Serves 8

BUTTER FOR GREASING

2 TABLESPOONS ORANGE LIQUEUR

600G CREAM CHEESE, AT ROOM TEMPERATURE

180G CASTER SUGAR

3 EGGS, LIGHTLY BEATEN

1 TEASPOON ORANGE FLOWER WATER

3 TABLESPOONS PLAIN WHITE FLOUR

FINELY GRATED ZEST OF 1 ORANGE

80G CANDIED FRUITS, FINELY CHOPPED

200G RASPBERRIES

ICING SUGAR TO DECORATE

Preheat the oven to 180°C/gas mark 4. Butter a 23cm springform cake tin.

In a large bowl, beat together the orange liqueur, cream cheese and caster sugar. Beat in the eggs bit by bit until fully combined. Mix in the orange flower water, then add the flour and orange zest. Beat well until everything is combined. Fold through the candied fruits and raspberries.

Spoon the mixture into the prepared tin, tapping it against the work surface to remove any bubbles. Bake in the middle of the oven for 35 minutes until the edges of the cake are firm but the centre is still slightly wobbly. Set aside to cool for 30 minutes.

Run a sharp knife around the edge of the cake to loosen it, then remove it from the tin.

Serve with a little icing sugar sprinkled on top.

SOUFFLÉ DI BANANE E CIOCCOLATO

SOUFFLÉ DI BANANE E CIOCCOLATO

Banana and Chocolate Soufflé

In our family, the combination of chocolate and banana is a big winner, especially in pancakes or cupcakes, so I created this soufflé just for a change. It's really easy to prepare, and also works well with strawberries or raspberries.

~~~~~~~~~~~~~~~~~~~~

Serves 8

15G UNSALTED BUTTER, MELTED

4 TABLESPOONS COCOA POWDER

2 LARGE RIPE BANANAS

4 HEAPED TABLESPOONS NUTELLA CHOCOLATE SPREAD, OR HONEY IF PREFERRED

5 EGG WHITES

2 TABLESPOONS CASTER SUGAR

ICING SUGAR FOR DUSTING (OPTIONAL)

Preheat the oven to 200°C/gas mark 6.

Grease 8 ramekins with the melted butter. Sprinkle 1 tablespoon of the cocoa powder inside each one, coating the bottom and sides evenly. Discard any excess cocoa.

Place the bananas and Nutella in a food processor or blender and blitz to a smooth texture. Transfer to a large mixing bowl and set aside.

In a large, clean dry bowl, whisk the egg whites until they have formed soft peaks. Add the caster sugar and whisk again for about 1 minute.

Using a flexible spatula, fold half the egg whites into the banana and chocolate mixture. Once combined, very gently fold in the rest.

Divide the mixture equally between the ramekins, then place in the oven and bake for 15 minutes until risen.

Sprinkle the top with icing sugar if you wish and serve immediately.

TIRAMISU CON CILIEGE

CHERRY TIRAMISU

If I asked you to name one Italian dessert, I guarantee the vast majority would say tiramisu. However, not everybody likes the coffee that the biscuits are traditionally soaked in, so my version – inspired by a trip to the cherry orchards of Castello, where Ciro and his family grow wonderful fruit – uses liqueur instead. If making this for children, just leave out the booze and cook the cherries in a little water.

~~~~~~~~~~~~~~~~~~~~~~~~~~~~~~~~~~~

Serves 4

400G CHERRIES, PITTED AND HALVED

50G CASTER SUGAR

4 TABLESPOONS CHERRY OR AMARETTO LIQUEUR

8 SMALL MADELEINE CAKES OR SPONGE FINGER BISCUITS

2 TABLESPOONS CHOPPED TOASTED NUTS

For the mascarpone cream

2 EGG YOLKS

2 TABLESPOONS CASTER SUGAR

250G MASCARPONE CHEESE

2 TABLESPOONS CHERRY OR AMARETTO LIQUEUR

Heat the cherries, sugar and 2 tablespoons of the liqueur in a saucepan until the sugar has dissolved and the cherries are slightly softened and their skin starts to burst. Set aside to cool.

For the mascarpone cream, whisk the egg yolks and sugar in a bowl until pale. Beat in the mascarpone and 2 tablespoons of the liqueur.

Place a layer of cake in the bottom of 4 individual glasses. Spoon over a little of the remaining liqueur, then add a layer of the cooked cherries and their juices. Top with a layer of the mascarpone cream. Repeat the layering until you are nearly at the top of the glass, finishing with the cream.

Sprinkle the top with chopped nuts and chill for 2 hours before serving.

TIRAMISU CON CILIEGE

TORTA DI MELE E RABARBARO

Apple and Rhubarb Almond Frangipane Pudding

It must be at least 10 years ago that my mother-in-law, Elizabeth, gave me an old family recipe for almond apple pie. It was delicious, but inevitably I started tweaking it. Happily, I got the thumbs-up from her for this version, so I hope you enjoy it as much as we all do.

~~~~~~~~~~~~~~~~~~~~~~~~~~~~~~~~~~~~~~~

Serves 8

5 COOKING APPLES, ABOUT 1KG, PEELED AND CORED
80G DEMERARA SUGAR
400G RHUBARB, CUT INTO 1CM CHUNKS
1 TABLESPOON GROUND CINNAMON
3 EGGS
200G CASTER SUGAR
200G SALTED BUTTER, AT ROOM TEMPERATURE
200G GROUND ALMONDS
5 TABLESPOONS FLAKED ALMONDS
ICING SUGAR TO DECORATE
MASCARPONE CHEESE TO SERVE

Preheat the oven to 180°C/gas mark 4.

Cut the apples into large chunks. Place in a large saucepan with the demerara sugar and cook over a low heat for 3 minutes. Add the rhubarb and cinnamon and stir occasionally for about 5 minutes.

Pour the mixture into an ovenproof dish about 20 x 30cm and leave to cool for 30 minutes at room temperature.

Meanwhile, cream the eggs and caster sugar in a large bowl. Add the butter and ground almonds and mix to a smooth paste.

Spread the almond mixture over the fruit and cook in the centre of an oven for 30 minutes until golden brown.

Sprinkle over the flaked almonds and cook for a further 10 minutes.

Serve hot with icing sugar on top and a dollop of mascarpone cheese on the side.

TORTA DI MELE E RABARBARO

ZUCCOTTO PANETTONE E MARSALA

ZUCCOTTO PANETTONE E MARSALA

PANETTONE, CHOCOLATE AND MARSALA
FROZEN CAKE

This is such an impressive-looking dessert and makes a
great end to any kind of meal. You can be as creative as
you like in flavouring the cream. In previous experiments
I have mixed it with fruit, chocolate bits and pieces of
marshmallow, but frankly I prefer this simpler version.

~~~~~~~~~~~~~~~~~~~~~~~~~~~~

Serves 8

500ML DOUBLE CREAM

100G ICING SUGAR

150G GOOD-QUALITY CHOCOLATE
(70% COCOA SOLIDS), ROUGHLY
CHOPPED

150G HAZELNUTS, ROUGHLY CHOPPED

200ML MARSALA WINE

1KG PANETTONE

150ML COLD WATER

COCOA POWDER TO DECORATE

Pour the cream into a large bowl, sift in the icing sugar and whip until
fluffy. Add the chocolate, hazelnuts and 2 tablespoons of Marsala, then
refrigerate for 15 minutes.

Line a 1.5 litre bowl with a large sheet of cling film, allowing it to overhang
the sides. Cut the panettone into 1.5cm slices and use them to line the
bowl. Reserve those you don't need for a 'lid'.

Pour the remaining Marsala and the cold water into a separate bowl.
Brush three-quarters of this liquid evenly over the sponge.

Pour the cream mixture into the sponge-lined bowl and gently tap it on the
work surface to release any air bubbles. Cover the top with the remaining
panettone slices and brush with the remaining Marsala mixture.

Cover the bowl with the overhanging cling film and freeze overnight.
Transfer to the fridge at least 1 hour before serving.

Invert the cake onto a plate, dust with sifted cocoa powder and serve.

INDEX

almonds: apple and rhubarb almond frangipane
    pudding 282
  double baked biscuits with
    almonds 234-5
amaretti biscuits with crushed
    hazelnuts 233
anchovies: pizza topped with anchovies, garlic and
    oregano 105-7
  roasted peppers with anchovies and pine nuts 26
  spaghetti with anchovies, breadcrumbs and garlic 98
apple and rhubarb almond frangipane pudding 282
artichokes: four seasons pizza topped with ham,
    artichokes, mushrooms and black olives 120-2
asparagus: pea, asparagus and mint risotto 168
aubergines: baked ricotta and potato cake with roasted
    aubergine 177-9
  griddled aubergine, peppers and courgette marinated
    in garlic oil 224

Baileys panna cotta 274
banana and chocolate soufflé 279
BBQ whole fish in foil 188
beans: Italian bean stew 171
  Italian beans with rosemary on garlic toasts 40
  traditional Neapolitan bean soup 55
  see also individual types of bean
beef: fettucine with a succulent meat and red wine
    sauce 77
  Italian beef stew with yellow peppers and olives 146
  my Mother's lasagne 94-7
  pappardelle with meatballs 85
  rolled filled pasta with pesto and béchamel
    sauce 73-5
  steak with herby sauce 137
  thinly slices of beef with parsley oil dressing 144
beetroot: sliced beetroot with watercress and walnut
    pesto 215
biscuits 230-1
bread 230-1
  bruschetta 163
  bruschetta with sun-dried tomato pesto 16
  classic ciabatta bread 246-7
  flat bread with garlic and parsley 253-5
  focaccia with crispy pancetta and red onions 236-8
  panini 243-5
  picnic pie 42
  rolled focaccia stuffed with mozzarella and
    tomatoes 241-2
  rustic Tuscan style 239
  southern Italian loaf encrusted with fennel seeds 251-2
  spiced paper thin bread with tapenade 33-5
brill roasted with sweet pepper sauce 192
broccoli: orecchiette with broccoli, garlic and chilli 80
bruschetta 163
  with sun-dried tomato pesto 16

butternut squash: potato and butternut squash soup 63
  roasted butternut squash risotto with sage
    butter 165-7

cakes: chocolate cup cakes 273
  la caprese di zia Rita 263
calzone 126-7
carpaccio: of beef 144
  of beetroot 215
cheese: creamy Parmesan polenta 219
  folded pizza stuffed with mozzarella, basil, peppers
    and salami Napoli 126-7
  fresh pasta with chicken and Gorgonzola sauce 88
  marinated mozzarella balls 37
  mozzarella and Parma ham rolls 21
  pizza topped with mozzarella, olives, mushrooms and
    ham 108-10
  pizza topped with mozzarella, spinach, egg and
    Parmesan 111-13
  pizza topped with mozzarella, tomatoes and fresh
    basil 114-15
  potato dumplings with tomato and mozzarella 82-4
  rolled focaccia stuffed with mozzarella and
    tomatoes 241-2
  spaghetti with eggs, pancetta and pecorino
    Romano 79
  types of mozzarella 14
  'white' pizza topped with mozzarella, Gorgonzola,
    Parmesan and Fontina cheese 118-19
  see also mascarpone; ricotta
cherry tiramisu 280
chicken: classic chicken broth 56-7
  crispy chicken breast served with pizza sauce 153-5
  fresh pasta with chicken and Gorgonzola sauce 88
  tray-baked chicken with tomatoes and olives 140
  whole salt-baked chicken 138
chocolate: banana and chocolate soufflé 279
  chocolate and cinnamon ice cream 272
  chocolate cup cakes 273
  la caprese di zia Rita 263
  panettone, chocolate and Marsala wine frozen
    cake 285
ciabatta, classic 246-7
clams: pasta with clams, garlic and chilli 99
cocktail, limoncello 18
courgettes: fried crispy courgettes 226
  courgette frittata 183
  griddled aubergine, peppers and courgette
    marinated in garlic oil 224
couscous, herby 195
cured meats 14

desserts 258-85
dumplings, bread 171

eggs: courgette frittata with tomato salsa 183
  pizza topped with mozzarella, spinach, egg

and Parmesan 111–13
spaghetti with eggs, pancetta and pecorino
  Romano 79

fennel: fennel and rocket salad 190
  southern Italian loaf encrusted with fennel seeds 251–2
  warm new potatoes, green beans and fennel 216
figs: warm figs stuffed with herb ricotta and wrapped
  in pancetta 39
fish 186–205
  BBQ whole fish in foil 188
  My Grandfather's special spicy fish soup 60
  Sicilian fish stew 203
  see also individual types of fish
focaccia: rolled focaccia stuffed with mozzarella and
  tomatoes 241–2
  with crispy pancetta and red onions 236–8
four seasons pizza 120–2
frittata, courgette 183

garlic: flat bread with garlic and parsley 253–5
  garlic bread 52–4
  orecchiette with broccoli, garlic and chilli 80
gnocchi: ricotta gnocchi with tomatoes and basil 175–6
  with tomato and mozzarella sauce 82–4
green beans: warm new potatoes, green beans and
  fennel 216
gremolata 143

ham: croquette potatoes with ham and Parmesan
  cheese 45
  four seasons pizza 120–2
  mozzarella and Parma ham rolls 21
  pizza topped with mozzarella, olives, mushrooms
  and ham 108–10
herbs: herby borlotti beans with olive oil
  breadcrumbs 220
  herby sauce 137

ice cream: chocolate and cinnamon 272
  easy strawberry 268
  limoncello 267
Italian bean stew 171
Italian beans with rosemary on garlic toasts 40
Italian beef stew with yellow peppers and olives 146

lamb: lamb cutlets with a honey and rosemary sauce 134
  slow-roasted leg of lamb stuffed with fennel seeds
  and apricots 150–2
lemons: chilli and lemon mayonnaise 31–2
  fresh lemon and lime sorbet 271
  lemon and basil dressing 177–9
  lemon and limoncello mousse 264
lentils: Italian sausages with braised lentils 159
  slow cooked 211
limes: fresh lemon and lime sorbet 271
limoncello: lemon and limoncello mousse 264

limoncello cocktail 18
limoncello ice cream 267

mascarpone: cherry tiramisu 280
  easy strawberry ice cream 268
  lemon and limoncello mousse 264
meatballs, pappardelle with 85
meats, cured 14
minestrone 52–4
mousse, lemon and limoncello 264
mushrooms: baked savoury pancakes with mushrooms,
  spinach and basil pesto 180–1
  four seasons pizza 120–2
  pizza topped with mozzarella, olives, mushrooms and
  ham 108–10
mussels: steamed mussels with chilli white wine and
  garlic 201

olives: four seasons pizza 120–2
  pizza topped with mozzarella, olives, mushrooms
  and ham 108–10
  tray-baked chicken with tomatoes and olives 140
onion, tomato and pancetta soup 51
oranges: raspberry and orange baked cheesecake 276

pancakes: baked savoury pancakes with mushrooms,
spinach and basil pesto 180–1
pancetta 14
  focaccia bread with crispy pancetta 236–8
  onion, tomato and pancetta soup 51
  spaghetti with eggs, pancetta and pecorino
  Romano 79
  warm figs stuffed with herb ricotta and wrapped in
  pancetta 39
panettone, chocolate and Marsala wine frozen cake 285
pangrattato, spicy 204
panini 243–5
panna cotta, Baileys 274
pasta 66–99
peas: fresh pea and basil creamy soup 58
  pea, asparagus and mint risotto 168
  scallops with pea purée and spicy pangrattato 204
peppers: folded pizza stuffed with mozzarella, basil,
  peppers and salami Napoli 126–7
  griddled aubergine, peppers and courgette marinated
  in garlic oil 224
  Italian beef stew with yellow peppers and olives 146
  roasted peppers with anchovies and pine nuts 26
  roasted tomato and pepper sauce 22–5
  sweet pepper sauce 192
pesto: baked savoury pancakes with mushrooms,
spinach
  and basil pesto 180–1
  rolled filled pasta with pesto and béchamel
  sauce 73–5
  sun-dried tomato 16
  walnut 215

picnic pie 42
pistachio nuts: la caprese di zia Rita 263
pizza 102-27, 163
polenta, creamy Parmesan 219
pomegranates: rocket, pine nut and pomegranate
   salad 222
pork: fettucine with a succulent meat and red wine
   sauce 77
   Italian sausages with braised lentils 159
   juicy roasted pork loin in milk and rosemary 147
   slow-roasted pork belly with radicchio 156
potatoes: baked ricotta and potato cake 177-9
   croquette potatoes with ham and Parmesan
      cheese 45
   potato and butternut squash soup 63
   potato dumplings with tomato and mozzarella 82-4
   roasted rosemary, garlic and olive oil potatoes 212
   scallops with pea purée and spicy pangrattato 204
   warm new potatoes, green beans and fennel 216
   warm potato salad 196
prawns: griddled prawns and squid with chilli and lemon
   mayonnaise 31-2
   marinated prawns and ciabatta kebabs with fennel
      salad 190
   My Grandfather's special spicy fish soup 60

radicchio, slow roasted pork belly with 156
raspberry and orange baked cheesecake 276
rhubarb: apple and rhubarb almond frangipane
   pudding 282
rice: pea, asparagus and mint risotto 168
   rice balls with roasted tomato and pepper sauce 22-5
   risotto 163
   roasted butternut squash risotto with sage
      butter 165-7
ricotta: baked ricotta and potato cake with roasted
   aubergine 177-9
   ravioli filled with smoked salmon and ricotta 91
   ricotta and spinach potato dumplings 175-6
   warm figs stuffed with herb ricotta and wrapped in
      pancetta 39
rocket: fennel and rocket salad 190
   rocket, pine nut and pomegranate salad 222

salads 208-27
salami, folded pizza stuffed with mozzarella, basil,
   peppers and 126-7
salmon: ravioli filled with smoked salmon and
   ricotta 91
   spicy tomato sauce with salmon, red chillies and
      garlic 70-2
salsa, tomato and caper 191
sardines: griddled sardines with warm potato salad 196
sauces: béchamel 73-5, 94-7
   herby 137
   honey and rosemary 134
   parsley and garlic 143

roasted tomato and pepper 22-5
   sweet pepper 192
sausages: Italian sausages with braised lentils 159
scallops with pea purée and spicy pangrattato 204
sea bass: BBQ whole fish in foil 188
   crispy fillet of sea bass with herby couscous 195
seafood: linguine with seafood sauce with chilli and
   white wine 92-3
   see also individual types
Sicilian fish stew 203
sorbet, fresh lemon and lime 271
soufflé, banana and chocolate 279
soups 48-63
spiced paper thin bread with tapenade 33-5
spinach: baked savoury pancakes with mushrooms,
   spinach and basil pesto 180-1
   pizza topped with mozzarella, spinach, egg and
      Parmesan 111-13
   ricotta and spinach potato dumplings 175-6
squid: griddled prawns and squid with chilli and lemon
   mayonnaise 31-2
stews: Italian bean 171
   Italian beef stew with yellow peppers and olives 146
   Sicilian fish 203
strawberries: easy strawberry ice cream 268

tapenade 33-5
tiramisu, cherry 280
tomatoes: courgette frittata with tomato salsa 183
   onion, tomato and pancetta soup 51
   potato dumplings with tomato and mozzarella 82-4
   roasted tomato and pepper sauce 22-5
   rolled focaccia stuffed with mozzarella and
      tomatoes 241-2
   spicy tomato sauce with salmon, red chillies and
      garlic 70-2
   sun-dried tomato pesto 16
   tomato and caper salsa 191
   tray-baked chicken with tomatoes and olives 140
tuna: griddled tuna steaks with tomato and caper
   salsa 191

veal: braised veal shanks with parsley and garlic
   sauce 143
vegetables: grilled 164
   minestrone 52-4
   pizza topped with sautéed vegetables 123-5
   roasted vegetables with thyme and honey 225
   see also individual types of vegetable

watercress: sliced beetroot with watercress and
   walnut pesto 215
wine: fettucine with a succulent meat and red wine
   sauce 77